Witnessing the Holocaust

Perspectives on the Holocaust

A series of books designed to help students further their understanding of key topics within the field of Holocaust studies.

Published:

Holocaust Representations in History, Daniel H. Magilow and Lisa Silverman
Postwar Germany and the Holocaust, Caroline Sharples
Anti-Semitism and the Holocaust, Beth A. Griech-Polelle
The Holocaust in Eastern Europe, Waitman Wade Beorn
The United States and the Nazi Holocaust, Barry Trachtenberg

Forthcoming:

Sites of Holocaust Memory, Janet Ward

Witnessing the Holocaust

Six Literary Testimonies

Judith M. Hughes

BLOOMSBURY ACADEMIC
LONDON • NEW YORK • OXFORD • NEW DELHI • SYDNEY

BLOOMSBURY ACADEMIC
Bloomsbury Publishing Plc
50 Bedford Square, London, WC1B 3DP, UK

BLOOMSBURY, BLOOMSBURY ACADEMIC and the Diana logo are trademarks of
Bloomsbury Publishing Plc

First published in Great Britain 2018

A catalogue record for this book is available from the British Library.

A catalog record for this book is available from the Library of Congress.

ISBN: HB: 978-1-3500-5858-3
PB: 978-1-3500-5857-6
ePDF: 978-1-3500-5859-0
eBook: 978-1-3500-5860-6

Series: Perspectives on the Holocaust

Typeset by Newgen KnowledgeWorks Pvt. Ltd., Chennai, India

To find out more about our authors and books visit www.bloomsbury.com
and sign up for our newsletters.

In memory of my husband, Stuart,
and
for my grandchildren, Jesse and Sophia

Contents

Preface

I want to head off a potential misunderstanding. Because I am both a psychoanalyst and a historian, when I first presented material from this project, my colleagues took it for granted that I would interpret the psyches of my protagonists. I may have disappointed them. I appreciate the wish for some kind of closure and the anxiety that comes from not being able to wrap up survivors' stories into neat—and possibly edifying—packages. But I can neither satisfy the wish nor banish the anxiety.

A second potential misunderstanding concerns my choice of authors. At the outset, I decided to focus on secular Jews. This was a matter of personal preference and also a matter of personal identification. Only as I was nearing the end of the study did I come to recognize another characteristic I share with my protagonists: an aversion to sentimentality. I have to assume that this dislike helped guide my initial selection.

My most recent book—*The Holocaust and the Revival of Psychological History*—grew out of an undergraduate seminar that I taught for a number of years. This one grew out of the same course—in a roundabout way. In the fall of 2013, when the earlier book was already under review, I had the impression that the students' attitude, at least in the beginning, could be summed up as: "War. Bad things happen." I was appalled by what I took to be, perhaps unfairly, a trivialization of the Holocaust. This new book may serve as an antidote. And it is all the more urgent to pay heed to the voices of survivors when the White House can release a statement on International Holocaust Remembrance Day, as it did in 2017, without even mentioning the Jews.

* * *

On two occasions I profited from feedback to lectures I gave when the project was in its initial stage. I presented material from Chapter 1 to the Holocaust Living History Workshop and material from Chapter 2 to the Department of History, both at the University of California, San Diego.

For decades I have talked to Donald L. Kripke and Edward N. Lee about psychoanalytic matters of mutual interest. On a number of evenings, we discussed autobiographies of Holocaust survivors, four of which I ended up including in this book. I much appreciated their responses to the texts and their shrewd observations. There are others who, over the years, have been ready listeners or willing readers. I would like to thank Frank Biess, Sandra Dijkstra, Joel Dimsdale, Margrit Frölich, Peter Gourevitch, Corey Robin, Stephen A. Schuker, Robert S. Westman, and my son, David. In the final stages, anonymous reviewers on behalf of Bloomsbury provided helpful suggestions.

Introduction

In 2005 the eighty-one-year-old writer Jorge Semprún addressed his fellow Buchenwald survivors and declared: "The cycle of active memory is closing."[1] A decade on, history, not memory, has become the instrument of recall. And here lies a danger—the danger of normalization and/or domestication. The very enormity of the crimes committed by the Nazis—their sheer implausibility—increases the likelihood of a leveling or flattening out. To prevent that, to preserve a sense of unease, of estrangement and of moral concern, one needs to hear the voices of those who experienced history in person. The cycle of memory may have closed, but the door to diaries and autobiographies remains open.

The voices I have in mind are those of Victor Klemperer, Ruth Kluger, Michał Głowiński, Primo Levi, Imre Kertész, and Béla Zsolt, My aim is to allow these survivors to speak, to sort out what was happening or had happened to them. I have tried to be attentive to the vivid detail of everyday life—without rushing to comment or interpret. To put it another way, I have undertaken to listen—keeping my presence in the narrative to a minimum. I have accepted my protagonists' compelling, albeit implicit, invitation to join them in their worlds—to be sure, as they have represented them. In so doing I have been mindful of their refusal to allow themselves to be erased, of their determination to provide a literary trail to ensure that those persecuted will not become nameless and faceless numbers.

Why these writers and not others? How to justify my choices? First, the authors I have selected are prominent, some very prominent, and, either in the original or in translation, their works are readily available to an English-speaking audience. Second, with the exception of Klemperer who converted to Protestantism as a young adult, they all are, or were, secular Jews. So Elie Wiesel is not in my cast of characters. And aside from Levi, my protagonists were not part of an organized resistance movement—and Levi was classified, by the Nazis, as a Jew and suffered accordingly. Thus Semprún and Charlotte Delbo have not been included.

The texts run from Klemperer's diary to Kertész's autobiographical fiction. Chronology and geography—the chronology and geography of the Nazis' expansion and the pursuit of their genocidal project, not blurry genre distinctions, govern the order of chapters. Klemperer, an inveterate diarist, remained in Dresden and kept track of the regime from start to finish. The Viennese-born Kluger was seven years old when Hitler annexed Austria in March 1938; four years later she was shipped first to Theresienstadt and then to Auschwitz. Głowiński was just turning five as the German army overran Poland in September 1939; after he and his parents escaped from the Warsaw ghetto, the boy found shelter in a Catholic convent. Not until September 1943 did the Germans invade Italy; shortly thereafter Levi was captured and transported to Monowitz-Buna, a satellite camp of Auschwitz. The Hungarian Jews were the last to fall prey to the Nazis—in March 1944; Kertész and Zsolt were rounded up, the former landed in Buchenwald, the latter contrived to escape. Taken together, these texts achieve my purpose: to convey a broad range of horrors.[2]

To bear witness—to preserve the memory of the Nazi onslaught—is the overarching theme. Others emerge along the way: time—how the sequencing in time helps; resourcefulness—albeit intermittent at best; and luck— all my protagonists insist on the role of chance. There is no sentimentality, and there is no pretense that one can salvage a tribute to the human spirit.

Some reflections on autobiography are in order. And these remarks cover diaries and autobiographical fiction as well. A reader might easily wonder: Isn't it all fiction? As a way to establish a boundary between factual and fictional modes of discourse, Philippe Lejeune, an eminent literary critic, proposed the notion of an autobiographical pact, a form of contract between author and reader in which the autobiographer commits himself to a sincere effort to come to terms with and to understand his own life. Lejeune conceived of this commitment not as something to be found in an author's psyche but as something to be found in the text.[3] In similar vein, Clifford Geertz, the most prominent anthropologist of his generation, drew attention to the question of how ethnographers persuade readers that "what they say is a result of their having actually penetrated … another form of life, of having one way or another, truly 'been there.'" As Geertz expressed it, for an ethnographer to be a "convincing 'I-witness,'" he must be a convincing "I," that is, the account becomes believable because the author/narrator has become credible. And again, the issue is not psychological; it is literary.[4]

Which brings me to a further point. One is predisposed to praise books by Holocaust survivors—indeed no record of that most terrible experience is without value. Yet the fact is that the quality of writing does count. To have witnesses, and survivors, who are also superb writers—that is the rare combination that sets my protagonists apart. So I have made extensive use of quotation. The reader needs to hear a good deal from the authors selected for the distinct flavor of their prose to emerge with force.

Finally, what am I expecting, hoping for, from the reader? Some familiarity with the writers canvassed? No. Some very general knowledge of and interest in the Holocaust? Yes. The Holocaust involved millions, but it was, as Kluger remarked, "a unique experience for each of them." All the protagonists in this study would have agreed with her when she admonished her readers to listen to her, absorb her story as she tells it, and "remember it."[5]

"Everything I Considered UnGerman ... Flourishes Here": Victor Klemperer

In 1995, Aufbau-Verlag, a struggling East German publishing house, brought out Victor Klemperer's diary covering the Nazi years, 1933–45. By then Klemperer had been dead for a quarter of a century. After his death, his second wife and widow had deposited the manuscript in the Saxon state archive. In the 1980s, along with a former student of her husband, she set to work deciphering and transcribing the original text of approximately 5,000 pages. When the edited version finally came out in Germany, it was a sensation. Despite its formidable size—roughly 1,700 pages—and its steep price—98DM—in the year after its publication, it sold 125,000 hardcover copies and remained on German best-seller lists for forty weeks.[1]

In 1998–99 a two-volume abridged English translation appeared—to an especially warm response. As Peter Gay commented, "To read Klemperer's almost day-by-day account is a hypnotic experience; the whole, hard to put down, is a true murder mystery—from the perspective of the victim." Gay continued—and this item he highlighted: "The true surprise" of the diary is "the number of 'good Germans' to whom he [Klemperer] gives an honorable place." The number is "astonishingly large." In "Klemperer's experience episodes of meanness and cowardice are far outweighed by moments of decency." Such instances, "literally dozens of gems," cumulatively refute "Daniel Goldhagen's thesis that Germans as a people were infected with 'eliminationist anti-Semitism.' "[2] In a similar vein, Gordon Craig claimed: "We find here much to indicate how far short Nazi propaganda fell from convincing ordinary Germans that the Jews were the source of all their problems."[3] Omer Bartov disagreed: "The argument made by many German and American reviewers of Klemperer's diaries, according to which German society did not turn against the Jews, is ... based on a highly selective reading of the text."[4] Highly selective—and tendentious. In other words, on the basis of these volumes alone, one cannot pronounce dogmatically on the anti-Semitism of ordinary Germans.

Born in 1881 in Landsberg on the Warthe, then in the eastern part of the Prussian province of Brandenburg (now the Polish town of Gorzow Wielkopolski), Klemperer was the ninth—and youngest—child of a reform rabbi. When he was nine, his father, after an unhappy stint with the Orthodox congregation of Bromberg (today Bydgoszcz), was appointed second preacher of the Berlin Reform Congregation—in the assimilationist parlance of the time, his father was referred to as a Landprediger (country preacher). Observance at the Reform Synagogue was extremely liberal: the services were held on Sundays and conducted almost entirely in German; heads were not covered, and men and women sat together; there were neither Sabbath restrictions nor dietary prescriptions; and instead of a bar mitzvah, boys and girls, at the age of fifteen or sixteen, were confirmed together on Easter Sunday. "The Reform Synagogue can perhaps be regarded as something of a halfway house to conversion to Protestantism." And Klemperer's three older brothers converted (his sisters did not); indeed they seemed to go "out of their way to deny their Jewish origins."[5] They urged Klemperer to do likewise, and in 1903 he took their advice.

Klemperer's brothers were a great trial to him. Georg, the eldest and Klemperer's senior by sixteen years, dominated the family. While still only in his thirties, he was on his way to a brilliant career as a physician. (In the early 1920s, Soviet authorities called him in to treat Lenin.) The two other brothers distinguished themselves as well, Felix also as a doctor, Berthold as a lawyer. None of them lived through the Third Reich in Germany. By 1933 Felix and Berthold were dead; and in 1935 Georg immigrated to the United States. Klemperer never shook the feeling that Georg stayed in touch—and helped him financially—only out of a sense of obligation to look after a sibling, despite the fact that he regarded his younger brother as something of a dilettante.

And with reason. Twice Klemperer interrupted his academic work: the first time to become an apprentice in a commercial enterprise—this proved a dead end; the second to become a writer and freelance journalist—here he had a modicum of success. But not enough—and not enough to make a living. Georg and Berthold prodded him—and offered financial assistance—to complete his doctoral studies. They made it clear to him that they would much prefer a professor to a journalist in their immediate family.[6] Klemperer complied and finished the work for his degree in 1913.

Klemperer's professorship—in 1920 he was named to a chair in romance literature at Dresden Technical University—brought him financial independence but little glory. In the 1920s he made repeated—and fruitless—efforts to get a post at a proper, older, and more prestigious university. His sort of scholarship played a role: his books on modern French prose and poetry, his history of French literature from Napoleon to the present, his study of Montesquieu, his biography of Corneille were marked by lucidity rather than originality. So too anti-Semitism played a role: being a Jew or an ex-Jew was still a handicap in the academy in Weimar Germany.

When on April 7, 1933—less than three months after Hitler came to power—the Law for the Restoration of the Professional Civil Service came into effect, Klemperer found himself at risk. Paragraph 3 stipulated that civil servants of non-Aryan origin were to retire—and Klemperer's conversion to Protestantism had not turned him into an Aryan. What saved him—in 1933—was his war service. (Klemperer had been called up in 1915 and had spent five months on the Western Front.) He noted his relief in his diary: "This awful feeling of 'Thank God, I'm alive.' The new Civil Service 'law' leaves me, as a front-line veteran, in my post—at least for the time being ... But all around rabble-rousing, misery, fear and trembling."[7]

Above all, Klemperer owed his survival to his first wife, Eva, a pianist and musicologist. They had married in 1906, and she died in 1951. Eva was, in Nazi jargon, a "full-blood Aryan," and her "racial purity" exempted her husband from deportation to the east and almost certain death. (In 1933, in the city and district of Dresden, the number of those registering as Jewish by confession stood at 4,675. At the beginning of February 1945, only 198 remained, a number that now included Klemperer.[8]) In the dedication to *LTI* (*Lingua tertii imperii*), his philological analysis of how the Nazis corrupted the German language and in so doing corrupted German thought, Klemperer expressed his gratitude to Eva: "But for you this book would not exist today, and its author, too, would have ceased to exist long ago." In the first chapter, he elaborated:

I know … of [a] kind of heroism … which is completely deprived of the support of being part of an army or a political group, of the hope of future glory, a heroism that was left to fend entirely for itself. These were the handful of Aryan wives (there were not many of them), who resisted every pressure to separate from their Jewish husbands. And just imagine what everyday life was like for these women! What insults, threats, blows … they endured … What a will to live they had to muster when they fell ill from all the humiliation and excruciating wretchedness … They knew that their death would inevitably be followed by that of their Jewish husband, because he would be [immediately] transported.[9]

As for his own heroism, it was in keeping a diary: it was "bearing witness," "precise witness!" After a house search by the Gestapo, Klemperer "found [that] several books … had been taken off the shelf [and were] lying on the desk. If one of them had been the Greek dictionary, if the manuscript pages had fallen out and had thus aroused suspicion, it would undoubtedly have meant" his death.[10] By 1942, Eva was periodically carrying pages of the diary to a devoted friend in Pirna.[11]

If making a record exposed Klemperer—and others—to grave danger, it also kept him more or less on an even keel.

Again and again during those years my diary was my balancing pole, without which I would have fallen down a hundred times. In times of disgust and despondency, … at the bedside of the sick and the dying, at grave-sides, at times when I myself was in dire straits, at moments of utter ignominy … —at all these times I was invariably helped by the demand that I had made on myself: observe, study and memorize what is going on.[12]

Readers of the diary know the outcome: they know about the atrocities the Nazi regime perpetrated—at least in a general way. But seeing them through the eyes of someone who was struggling to sort out and to face the realities of the situation brings these horrors home in a particularly poignant fashion.

"How completely homeless I am"

At this point, October 1, 1934, the move into our own house, whatever the circumstances, whatever my feelings, however different from what

I imagined, however bitter the memories and however great the worries—I shall one day begin my memoirs. If time is left me for them.[13]

While Jews were leaving Germany or beginning to think about leaving Germany, Klemperer was digging in—literally.[14]

In July 1932, as a birthday present to Eva, he had bought a plot of land in Dölzschen, a village on the outskirts of Dresden. Eva had blamed him—during moments of great distress—"for her ruined life ... because against her urgent wishes, her better judgment, her calculations and building plans," he had "hesitated with the construction." He acknowledged the justice of her complaints: he had resisted at first. "The burden and commitment seemed too great," his "inexperience in building matters too dangerous." So he had forced himself to act enthusiastically, "as if he ... believed in the building of the house"—and gradually, little by little, he actually did.[15]

Finances were a chronic problem. Klemperer's initial effort to secure building funds failed. Worse than that. The man whom he paid to locate a lender absconded with the finder's fee. (Raising mortgage money was not handled through a bank. It was usually a private transaction, that is, Klemperer needed to track down someone willing to lend at a fixed interest rate for a fixed term.) Unexpectedly he hit upon a solution—here was the "greatest irony"—thanks to a National Socialist law that compelled Germans to sell their foreign assets, with the government then taking the foreign exchange and paying in Reichsmarks. An acquaintance—someone Eva knew well enough to show the plot of land and explain the money troubles—had a property in England that had to be sold. She wanted to invest the repatriated funds and offered Klemperer a loan. A self-contained middle section of the whole house could now be built. One further—and "amusing"—difficulty: the building regulations of the Third Reich required "German" houses, and flat roofs were "un-German." "Fortunately Eva quickly found that she could like a gable, so the house" was topped off with "a 'German gable.' "[16]

It turned out that the German gable raised the cost. It also turned out that the house induced continual outlays. When, thanks to an interest-free loan from Georg, Klemperer had some cash, he spent a good deal of it on expanding the dwelling. "The little house," Klemperer wrote in September 1935, "is now a proper house, in fact a 'villa.' " Still Klemperer continued to build. His next project, undertaken in 1936 and paid for by borrowing against his life insurance, was a garage. It caused him "endless worry, trouble and annoyance." "A few weeks ago the usual shed with a flat roof, was completed here … But *I* am not allowed to build one. *This* year there must be no more *disfigurement*; they are demanding a pointed decorative roof, which would take space and view from us. At the District Office I told the clerk: 'I am not disfiguring anything. Then there will simply be no construction and no work.' … The next day the master mason and the carpenter go to the mayor and ask him [to reconsider] for the sake of their work. He gives them a message for me: I did not seem to know the way things were, I was a guest here, and he had a mind to take me into custody for a night … The whole business with the car seems ever more absurd."[17]

Klemperer had embarked on that project or rather had committed to driving lessons in a brief moment of "high spirits." In January 1936, after two courses of lessons, he passed the test. "This business," he commented, "is really a victory over my nature." Driving lessons, purchasing a second-hand car, building the garage were all "desperate actions—appropriate to the times." The car turned out to be another source of "endless worry, trouble and annoyance"—and expense. It "rules me," Klemperer groaned. It "never works properly, something is always failing, I have lost all confidence in it, [and] in the mechanics … I am always assured … that now everything is in perfect working order, and yet something goes wrong every time I drive. Fuel pump, starter, battery, brakes." Then there was his "wretched driving." The most difficult thing was getting in and out of his property. He repeatedly dented the mudguard, damaged the gate and the little garden wall. "One had to persevere," he told himself, "perhaps the pleasure" was yet "to come."[18]

It did come. But financial straits "often to the point of despair" made him keep the car in the garage more than he would have liked. (In late 1936 he was "delivered from the worst … by a quite unexpected and truly very moving present … from Georg." In the following years, he received other presents—no longer unexpected.) On one "very short drive"—short "for reasons of economy"—he and Eva found themselves, by chance, "on the new Reich autobahn from Wilsdruff to Dresden, less than an hour after it was opened. There were still flags and flowers from the ceremony …, a mass of cars moved slowly forward at a sightseeing pace … This straight road consisting of four broad lanes, each direction separated by a strip of grass, is magnificent. And bridges for people to cross over it. Spectators crowded onto these bridges and the sides of the road. A procession. And a glorious view … toward the Elbe and the Lössnitz Hills." They drove "the whole stretch and back again," and twice Klemperer "risked a speed of 50 mph."[19] In this—and other excursions as well—he took real delight.

The excursions, the driving, came to an abrupt end in the wake of Kristallnacht, the nationwide pogrom that took place on November 9–10, 1938.

> The healthy sense of justice of every German … ([an] evermore frequent phrase … always printed when some new atrocity is initiated) … manifested itself yesterday in a decree from Police Minister [Heinrich] Himmler with immediate effect: withdrawal of driving license from all Jews. Justification: Because of the Grünspan murder [Herschel Grynzspan's shooting of the German diplomat Ernst vom Rath] Jews are unreliable, are therefore not allowed to sit at the wheel, also their being permitted to drive offends the German traffic community, especially as they have presumptuously made use of the Reich highways built by German workers' hands. This prohibition hits us terribly hard.

Gone was his "last piece of freedom."[20]

* * *

On April 30, 1935, Klemperer had received a dismissal notice through the mail. It read: "On the basis of para 6 of the Law for the Restoration of the Professional Civil Service I have … recommended your dismissal. Notice of dismissal enclosed." Signed Martin Mutschmann, Gauleiter of Saxony. (Note that Klemperer was not dismissed by virtue of paragraph 3, the so-called Aryan Paragraph.) Klemperer appreciated that his dwindling number of students had long since made him vulnerable. In November 1933 he had noted: "At the first lecture Monday, French Renaissance, five people; for the exercises, Renaissance lyric poetry, four; today at Corneille, two … I must now reckon seriously with the withdrawal of my chair." And so he was forced into retirement, not as a Jew but as "superfluous."[21] (He received a pension of roughly 60 percent of his salary, though over time the regime enacted various ingenious deductions. In November 1943 the pension payments stopped entirely.)

As Klemperer put it in his *LTI*, after his dismissal, he buried himself in his scholarly work.

> At the outset while I was still suffering no persecution, or at most a very mild form, … I buried myself in my profession, I gave my lectures and desperately ignored the increasingly yawning gaps in the rows of seats in front of me, I exerted all my energies on my eighteenth century French literature … When the civil service was purged and I no longer had my lectern to lean on, my initial reaction was to try to cut myself off from the present entirely. Those thoroughly unmodern Enlightenment thinkers, long since despised by anybody who thought they were anybody, had always been my favourites—Voltaire, Montesquieu and Diderot. I could now dedicate all my time and energy to my opus which was already well advanced; as far as the eighteenth century was concerned I was in clover in the Japanese Palace in Dresden; no German library, and perhaps not even the national library in Paris, could have served me better.[22]

But then, in December 1938, shortly after Kristallnacht, came the ban on the use of the library—the reading room had been closed to him more than two years earlier—"pulling," he wrote, "my life's work away from under me."[23]

* * *

Kristallnacht: Klemperer saw no need to "describe the historic events …, the acts of violence … Only the immediately personal and what concretely affected us." So he took pains to record the house search to which he and Eva had been subjected.

> On the morning of … [November] eleventh, two policemen accompanied by a "resident of Dölzschen." Did I have any weapons?—Certainly my saber, perhaps even my bayonet as a war memento, but I wouldn't know where.—We have to help you find it … At the beginning Eva made the mistake of quite innocently telling one of the policemen he should not go through the clean linen cupboard without washing his hands. The man, considerably affronted, could hardly be calmed down. A second, younger policeman was more friendly, the civilian was the worst … They rummaged through everything, chests and wooden constructions Eva had made were broken open with an ax. The saber was found in a suitcase in the attic, the bayonet was not found … At about one o'clock the civilian and the older policeman left the house, the young one remained.… [He ordered:] "You must dress and come to the court building at Münchner Platz with

me." ... I was allowed to shave (with the door half open), I slipped Eva some money, and we made our way to the tram ...; the policeman kindly covered up the fact that I was being taken into custody. A wing of the court building: Public Prosecutor. A room with clerks and policemen. Sit down ... I sat there ... Waiting. After a while a young man with the Party badge appeared, evidently the examining Magistrate. You are Professor Klemperer? You can go. But first of all a certificate of discharge had to be made out, otherwise the police ... will think you have escaped and arrest you again ... At four o'clock I was on the street ... with the curious feeling, free—but for how long?

Klemperer's initial response to his arrest was to send an urgent SOS to Georg, now settled in the United States. The short letter began: "With a heavy heart, in a quite altered situation, pushed right to the edge, no details: Can you stand surety for my wife and myself, can you help the two of us over there for a couple of months?"[24]

Georg cabled back immediately: "Assume surety." Klemperer promptly took himself to the American consulate—a necessary first step in the complex process of emigration. He reported back to his brother: "Large, elegantly furnished offices ... After some back and forth received by a younger black-haired gentleman. Handshake, courtesy. He could not speak a word of German, called a blond Dr. Dietrich (introduction, handshake) as interpreter; then it turned out that the consul spoke Italian ... [Klemperer did too] so there was a curious mixture of languages. Result: no hope, it is not even possible to register me as a professor because for that I would have to have been dismissed for two years at most, but not as long ago as 1935. I told the story of my saber etc." Three months later he and Eva did receive waiting-list numbers from the American consulate in Berlin: 56,429 and 56,430.[25]

By early 1939 Klemperer had come to the conclusion that the prospect of getting American visas was zero. By 1941, when there was a chance that his and Eva's quota numbers might be reached in the course of the year, all his ambivalence—indeed aversion—to leaving Germany resurfaced: "I dread the thought of the USA. Dependent on Georg and his sons, not knowing the language, ... and 60 years old." It was almost with relief that he reported, in July, that further regulations rendered their affidavits invalid: "The new procedure means effectively that it will be impossible to get out in any foreseeable future … All vacillation is now at an end. Fate will decide."[26]

This invocation of fate was a familiar trope. It went hand in hand with Klemperer's reluctance, his resistance, to the very idea of emigration. When such a thought intruded, he quickly mobilized two considerations to banish it again. First, his professional inadequacy. In 1933, when friends started to get out, he judged himself to be a "completely useless … creature of over-refinement." His friends, he lamented, could "earn a living here and there," could "somehow switch to practical things … I cannot even be a language teacher … I only lecture on the history of ideas, and only in German." Second, Eva. In 1935, after he was dismissed from his academic post, he engaged in a flurry of letter writing. To what end he wondered? "Eva has been recently suffering a great deal again—repeated dental treatment, root inflammation, general nervous strain—according to her, … she would be a prisoner in any pension or furnished or city apartment." And, in 1941, when he was musing on whether to try to expedite their emigration, he had a "long painful consultation" with his wife. "She said, over there she would only be able to sit around and go to the cinema, nothing else. *Here* at least she retained some hope … We shall do nothing to speed it up and continue to wait and see as 'obstinately' as before."[27]

By then, they were no longer in their own home. In May 1940, eight months after the outbreak of the Second World War, as the German army was overrunning France, the Klemperers were forced to move into a Jews' house—the first of three in which they lived before the bombing of Dresden. They were compelled to rent out their house to a grocer who proceeded to set up his shop in the Klemperers' music room. Over the next four plus years, Klemperer was dunned for all sorts of alterations and repairs: the roof, for example, in order to fit in with its surroundings—it wasn't enough that it had a gable—had to be covered with "red bricks or red imitation slate" instead of tar board; the rubble that resulted from the grocer's remodeling had to be removed—and Klemperer had to pay for it; and the whole house and the big veranda had to be painted and completely renovated to keep them from going to rack and ruin. But when the grocer, who initially seemed a "very decent man, … soldier and NCO in the World War," subsequently a Nazi "political officer," tried to buy the house, Klemperer refused and managed to scrape together the funds to make his refusal stick.[28]

* * *

Palestine never figured in Klemperer's half-hearted attempts to emigrate. In July 1933, he reported: "We hear a lot about Palestine now; it does not appeal to us. Anyone who goes there exchanges nationalism and narrowness for nationalism and narrowness." Klemperer was anti-Zionist and passionately so. "To me the Zionists, who want to go back to the Jewish state of A.D. 70 (destruction of Jerusalem by Titus) are just as offensive as the Nazis. With their nosing after blood, their ancient 'cultural roots,' ... they are altogether a match for the National Socialists." That was 1934. In late 1939, anticipating his move into a Jews' house, he noted that "Jewish communities in Germany today" were now "all extremely inclined to Zionism." For his part, "I shall go along with that just as little as I do with National Socialism ... Liberal and German *forever.*"[29]

Klemperer's equation of Zionism and Nazism did not persist. (How could it have, as he began to appreciate Hitler's exterminationist project?) His commitment to "Germanness" did, and he agonized again and again about it. Within weeks of Hitler's assuming the chancellorship, he commented: "Everything I considered un-German, brutality, injustice, hypocrisy, mass suggestion to the point of intoxication, all of it flourishes here." A year later he added: "The dreadful thing is that a European nation has delivered itself up to such a gang of lunatics and criminals and still puts up with them." All the while he kept posing a painful question: "Has Germany really become so ... fundamentally different, has its soul changed so completely that this will endure?" The fact is, he wrote in late 1936, "the Nazi is in part not really alien to the people, in part is gradually polluting the healthy section of the population."[30] Months before Kristallnacht—months before "Hitler, Göring, and their associates entirely destroyed any remaining possibility for Jewish life in Germany or for the life of Jews in Germany"[31]— Klemperer expressed his anguish: "How deeply Hitler's attitudes are rooted in the German people, how good the preparations were for his Aryan doctrine, how unbelievably I have deceived myself my whole life long, when I imagined myself to belong to Germany, and how completely homeless I am."[32]

And yet he still managed to cling to his notion of Germanness—rooted, paradoxically enough, in the French Enlightenment: "No one can take my Germanness away from me, but my nationalism and patriotism are gone forever. My thinking is now completely Voltairean cosmopolitanism ... Voltaire and Montesquieu are more than ever my essential guides."[33]

"Murder is ... at our heels"

On the morning of May 16, 1940, the Klemperers moved into the Jews' house at 15B Caspar David Friedrich Strasse. "A handsome villa, too cramped, too 'modern' in style, stuffed full of people, who all share the same fate." Two rooms had been assigned to him and Eva. "Tangled chaos in both ... Still quite impossible to know whether a tolerable existence can be established here." When in September 1942, he was forced to relocate again, he vowed: "As far as it lies in my power, the Jews' House at 15B Caspar David Friedrich Strasse and its many victims will be famous."[34]

From first to last, Klemperer complained about losing time—a loss caused by the "constant fussing interference" of his housemates. (Unable to continue his research and writing on the eighteenth century, he was drafting his memoirs and studying the language of the Third Reich and, of course, keeping his diary.) Frau Kätchen Voss ranked as the principal "fussbudget." Somewhere in her fifties, she was the "very well-to-do non-Aryan widow of the Aryan director of the Public Insurance Institute of Saxon Savings Banks (formerly a Catholic priest)." A "somewhat childish, barely educated, somewhat petty bourgeois woman, good-natured, helpful," she was also "very much in need of company, tremendously talkative." From morning until midnight, she was at hand or rather under foot. "Early in the morning she's sitting by Eva's bed, she is there at every meal, she never stops talking." But for all her "blathering," Klemperer counted her a useful informant, particularly after she started working at the Zeiss-Ikon plant in late 1941. (She was doing labor service "'voluntarily' because that is supposed to provide protection against deportation"—it did not—"also voluntarily without quotation marks, because it's like bridge, all her male and female friends work there.") At Zeiss-Ikon, Klemperer remarked, "they always know everything, and sometimes it's even true."[35]

Frau Voss was Klemperer's co-tenant and lived on the same floor. The owner, Ernst Kreidl, and his Aryan wife, Elsa, occupied the floor above them. He was "a friendly man (over sixty) good storyteller, she (much younger)" was unpleasant and "bitter at being stuck in the Jewish schlamassel." With Kreidl, Klemperer traded assessments of the political situation, how the war was going, how long the Nazi regime would last, what would be the fate of the Jews. (From one day to the next, their opinions—and mood—oscillated greatly.) Like Klemperer, Kreidl was devastated by the decree of September 1941 ordering Jews to wear a yellow star. For close to two months, he refused to leave the house. And then he was "summoned to the Gestapo ... 'for questioning,' did not come back ... In custody, political grounds. No one knows anything more." Klemperer counted the weeks as they went by, and still no further information was forthcoming. After five months in the Dresden police cells, Kreidl, so Klemperer learned, was sent to Buchenwald. A couple of weeks later, Klemperer heard "weeping and shouting above ... us. Immediate assumption: Elsa Kreidl will have received news of the death of her husband in the concentration camp. Whether this is so or not"—it was—"the fact that we and Käthchen [Frau Voss] immediately assumed it and consider it to be almost certain is the most characteristic thing about our situation."[36]

In February 1942, Frau Julia Pick moved in on the floor below. "A lady (really a lady) of 76," Klemperer wrote, "formerly well-off" (her late husband had some kind of very large malt factory), "now impoverished, family abroad. Uncommonly vigorous, full of the joys of life (very Austrian), yet her demeanor is at once hearty and dignified. She stroked my hand: 'You could be my son; in my day girls married at 16.'" The affection—and respect—was mutual. Following a house search by the Gestapo—the fourth in the space of two weeks—Klemperer reported on what had befallen her.

> She has ... been terribly beaten and knocked about. "Your husband had the malt factory. The bloodsucker! Your *litter* is abroad and inciting hatred against us, but we've got you, and you won't get away from us.—You will be at the Gestapo at seven o'clock tomorrow morning—you'll go alone— anyone accompanying you goes straight to a concentration camp." ... Frau Pick said she was physically incapable of going all that way to be ill-treated again, she had had a good life, and now it was over ... We were seriously concerned about her. At nine she came upstairs to see us, brought 55M,

some jewelry, and a couple of little things, we should have them if she were arrested tomorrow. Just before ten I went down to her again; she was sitting quietly in her leather armchair, a blanket pulled over her, very calm, but very pale, and there was a constant twitch between her eyes. I told her: "We won't pretend; you intend to kill yourself. Think about your children, think that where there's life, there's hope, that the Nazis' cause is hope*less*, stay brave …," etc., etc. I tried to give her strength in every way possible, to appeal to her. I said: "Give me your word you will do nothing to yourself."—"I cannot promise that, I will consider things once again."

The next morning, after looking in on Frau Pick—"the woman appeared to be sleeping calmly, but her breathing was very quiet"—Klemperer went across the road and telephoned for medical assistance.

When the nurse, a calm, mature woman, came, Frau Pick was still unconscious, but her breathing was better, she was also moving occasionally. It did not appear to be a serious poisoning … I saw and heard something of Frau Pick gradually coming to. Distressing … How, helpless and stupefied, she was placed on a chamber pot, how the naked thighs were yellow bones with a little covering, how through clumsiness the pot broke … I felt horror.

A couple of months later, Klemperer noted: "Frau Pick attempted suicide a second time, and this time successfully." Her name had been on the list of those to be deported to Theresienstadt.

Eva was first to go downstairs, at seven o'clock, and then told me, this time it was more serious, she was groaning loudly. I was downstairs a quarter of an hour later, by which time there was no sound anymore, mouth open, one eye open, obviously dead … Substitutes are listed in advance for every transport. The Gestapo takes it as certain that a number of suicides will occur. German organization.[37]

German organization had emptied out the house at Caspar David Friedrich Strasse: "la maison juive morte"—most of the inhabitants were gone, dead.[38]

* * *

On September 1, 1942, Klemperer noted that "the troubles and tribulations of the move" to 2 Lothringer Weg had begun. By the end of the month, he felt more or less settled. "All in all" he judged his "new lodgings" to be "preferable" to the old. The style, the "heavy, solid elegance of the grand bourgeois," was more to his liking. And the common kitchen, in the cellar, was "so large that no one disturbs anyone else ... One more thing: No one in the house is mockingly disapproving if I share in our housework. That is normal here and it is taken for granted, that each person does every kind of work. Every day I experience anew the feeling of relief that I am spared the accompaniment of Kätchen's [Frau Voss's] blathering while I am washing up.—Admittedly, however, I would have not have acquired such a precise knowledge of Jewish fates in Jews' House II."[39] (He did learn of Kätchen's fate: in late 1942, she was forced to move into the newly erected barracks at Hellerberg and from there she was deported. Klemperer did not seem to know that her final destination was Auschwitz.)

The following April he drew up a balance sheet—albeit a provisional one. "I feel my imprisonment ... keenly. It has become more and more constraining from year to year ... Today I am not ... allowed to use the tram, I am not allowed to step outside the city boundary, I am not allowed to be seen with Eva; since the latest arrests it is best not to be seen on the street at all. (At the very least I avoid the elegant city center, like all wearers of the star.)—I have spent all morning scrubbing the kitchen and am about to go downstairs again to make tea and wash up; of course I feel very depressed. Nevertheless I have *still* not been arrested, we have still to be given the threatened notice to leave ... I can still read ... for hours, still sit at my desk."[40]

Among his blessings, Klemperer counted a negative: he had not received the dreaded call-up for labor service. Within days of his diary entry, that changed: he was ordered to work, first in a tea factory and then in two different box factories. When, fourteen months later, he was finally "released from duty," he regarded it as "a historic date" in his life. Throughout those months he lamented his inept performance—at none of the tasks assigned to him was he any good—and the "wasted time." That said, he did encounter a new set of acquaintances, and it did him good, he acknowledged, "to be among people who are of the same age, or older, and are suffering more. I often tell myself: If all of these accept life, without staring at the death before them, or at the youth behind them, why should I not manage that too?"[41]

Those new acquaintances debated "passionately ... always ... about Germans and Jews."

> Müller is vehemently German, without being anti-Semitic, although he has an aversion to eastern Jews; he disputes the existence of a Jewish *race*, he disputes that the German people are universally anti-Semitic, he disputes that Hitler and his regime completely correspond to the character of the German people. Dr. Lang is very bitter; to him anti-Semitism is an ineradicable part of the German character, Hitler absolutely in conformity with the German character. Jacobi, who is muddleheaded and hardly altogether normal, and Witkowsky take up positions halfway between the two; I, in large part, agree with Müller.

KIemperer summed up: "*All* these people, the core of businessmen, the academic and proletarian wings, are separated from orthodox Jewry by mixed marriage. In some, the inclination to Germany ... is dominant ..., in others Judaism has retained or gained hold."[42]

Of one thing Klemperer became increasingly confident: "*The Jewish question is alpha and omega*." Each day taught him anew that for the Third Reich the war was really "the *Jewish War*"—and no one could "experience it as acutely and tragically as the star-wearing Jew ... who in his upbringing, education, and sentiments is truly German."[43]

* * *

The Klemperers changed house for a third time in December 1943. They, along with another family, were "put in the Hirschels' former apartment, 3 Zeughausstrasse." The Hirschels had been forced out of a "very elegant property" owned by the wife (the Gestapo had "bought" that property) and into rooms belonging to the Jewish community—he was the community superintendent. Within weeks of this relocation, Eva reported: "The Community has been sealed. No one answered the door." Klemperer wondered: "Have the last Jews not in mixed marriages been deported?"[44] (After the war, he learned that the Hirschel family, "taken from Theresienstadt to Auschwitz, had undoubtedly been completely exterminated, husband, wife, 2 boys."[45])

Hirschel, who had been well informed about the rise in deportations and deaths among the city's Jews, told Klemperer of an incident with a Gestapo inspector: "Clemens said, 'I hate you so much; rely on it, I'll finish you off.'

Hirschel who often has to negotiate with him, responded: 'Why do you hate me so much?' Clemens: 'I can tell you exactly. Because you're a Jew. I'll kill you for sure.' Hirschel also thought: Only quick change can save us." Everyone, Klemperer remarked, "but everyone, says the same thing, usually formulated in exactly the same way: 'They [the Nazis] are lost in the foreseeable future, utterly, but if things don't happen quickly—and it does not look as if they will—they will finish us off first.' Truly," he added, "murder is horribly at our heels as never before."[46]

Now, in a "mood of despair," Klemperer was moving to 3 Zeughausstrasse. Now he was "completely in the hands of the Gestapo, completely surrounded by Jews ... It is half like living in barracks," tripping "over one another higgledly-piggledy." And now, he added, when "the expected air raid comes, we ... are right in the center and in the city."[47]

* * *

The air raid, famous—or infamous—for the devastating fire storm it produced, took place on the night of February 13, 1945. Ten days later, Klemperer managed to write an account of how he and Eva escaped the conflagration. From then until June 1945, whenever they paused in their flight, he spent hours drafting, with great difficulty, a "supplement" to his diary: "the ink, paper, pen" he scrounged were "a torture to use."[48]

On that night, around 1 a.m., Eva said: "Air-raid warning ... It wasn't loud, they're going around with hand sirens, there's no electricity." The two of them hurried downstairs.

> The street was as bright as day and almost empty, fires were burning, ... [a] storm was blowing ... Eva was two steps ahead of me. We came to the entrance hall of no. 3 [Zeughausstrasse]. At that moment a big explosion nearby. I kneeled, pressing myself against the wall ... When I looked up Eva had disappeared. I thought she was in our cellar ... I ran across the yard to our Jews' cellar ... The door was wide open ... I called out several times to Eva. No reply ... Bangs, ... explosions. I had no thoughts, I was not even afraid, I was simply tremendously exhausted ... After a moment I scrambled over some vaulting or a stop or a parapet into the open air, ... lay flat on the ground ... Someone called out: "This way, Herr Klemperer!" ... A group of people were clambering up through the public gardens to the Brühl Terrace; the route was close to the fires, but it had to be cooler at the top and easier to

breathe. Then I was standing at the top in the storm wind and the showers of sparks ... Slowly thoughts came to me. Was Eva lost, had she been able to save herself, had I thought too little about her? ... Sometimes I thought: she is more capable and courageous than I am, she will have got to safety; sometimes: If at least she didn't suffer! Then again simply: If only the night were over! ... The burning went on and on ... Finally, probably at about seven the terrace—the terrace forbidden to Jews—was by now somewhat empty, I walked past the shell of the still-burning Belvedere and came to the terrace wall. A number of people were sitting there. After a minute someone called out to me: Eva was sitting unharmed on the suitcase wearing her fur coat ... At the critical moment, someone had literally pulled Eva out of the entry of no. 3 Zeughausstrasse and into the Aryan cellar, she had got out through the cellar window, had seen both numbers 1 and 3 completely alight, had been in the cellar of the Albertinum for a while, then reached the Elbe through the smoke, had spent the rest of the night partly looking for me ... Once, as she was searching, she had wanted to light a cigarette and had had no matches; something was glowing on the ground, she wanted to use it—it was a burning corpse ... So now it was Wednesday morning, February 14, and our lives were saved and we were together.[49]

Once reunited, Eva ripped the star from her husband's coat with a penknife. This "step was of necessity followed by others." In an army base to which the homeless of Dresden were evacuated, Klemperer registered as Victor Klemperer, not Victor-Israel Klemperer as the regime had mandated in August 1938. When food coupons were distributed, he signed the same way. In Piskowitz, where the Klemperers next took refuge, this time with a former maid, the young mayor, after taking down their information, asked: "'You are not of Jewish descent or of mixed race?' 'No.'" Still, they had to move on—there were too many refugees and too few accommodations. In Falkenstein, seeking shelter with an old friend, Klemperer continued to agonize: "If only the ever more strongly tormenting feeling of being hunted would disappear. I *have to* sit in a restaurant several times a day, and every minute is torture. (On the street, while walking ... I feel in general, not always—a little safer.) I look at every passing person, trying to judge whether he is a Party official or something similar."[50] Not until they were close to Munich and were welcomed by people they had merely heard of but had never met, did Klemperer's anxiety abate.

As refugees the Klemperers were eligible for requisitioned rooms, and by mid-April, after a great deal of trekking from office to office and town to town, all in the vicinity of the Bavarian capital, they found lodging in the village of Unterbernbach. When three weeks later the war came to an end, Klemperer determined to return to Dresden as soon as possible. "To get real help," he surmised, "I would have to reveal myself as a Jew. But," he added, "I would want to do that only when I can definitely ... leave my present surroundings." Within days he decided to risk it, within days he appeared before an official of the American military government in a neighboring town, actually before a "young woman with large, gray-blue eyes, not Jewish-looking, wearing very thick lipstick ... smoking cigarette after cigarette, talking animatedly in an Austrian accent." When the room grew emptier, Klemperer "told her in a low voice and in a few words," who he was, and pushed his "Jewish identity card over to her."

> Immediately smiling courtesy, helpfulness, expression of respect. One "Herr Professor" after another. Did I need financial help, did I have decent accommodation, clothing would be attended to, tomorrow she would have the mayor of Unterbernbach there, she would make a note of my name: "K—l—e—m—p—e—r—e—r," beaming: "I've heard of it"—she will no doubt have heard of Georg or Otto Klemperer [a famous conductor and cousin], nevertheless it was to my advantage.—"I shall talk to the mayor, Herr Professor!"—"Madam, I really would not like people in the village to find out." ... Vehemently: "Well, do you think you still have anything to fear?" ... I had nothing at all to fear ... Only I ... had to have patience with regard to departure.

Despite the many and various restrictions on travel, he and Eva decided to embark on what they appreciated was "a crazy enterprise: ... to cover two hundred or two hundred fifty miles, without proper hiking things, without any certainty about food-ration cards, about lodgings." Their odyssey lasted more than two weeks, most of it on foot—Klemperer had managed to have his shoes "excellently and thoroughly repaired" before setting out.[51] On June 10, tired and hungry, they reached Dresden.

Then the "fairy-tale turnabout came. The day began gloomily enough ... After an impossible night," they "walked right through all the destruction of the city center. In Theaterstrasse there was supposed to be an inquiry office with information about residents ... who had been bombed out. It was closed." They started to search, dragging themselves from place to place in hopes of locating people they had known. They discovered dwellings that were obliterated, leaving no trace of the former inhabitants. Finally they found the building where the Glasers—friends in a mixed marriage—lived. On the whole, it was "wonderfully preserved, with nothing but ruins all around ... Frau Glaser welcomed" them "with tears and kisses," she had thought them dead. They were fed; they were able to rest. In the late afternoon they "walked up to Dölzschen"—and reclaimed their house.[52]

Coda

The fairy tale lasted only a short time. In subsequent years Klemperer was named to a series of prestigious professorships; his study of Nazi language, *LTI*, was published and reprinted a number of times; he revised and reissued his older works; and he was elected to both the Volkskammer, the representative assembly of the German Democratic Republic, and to the Academy of Sciences. Yet the life that his postwar diaries depicts was not one of triumph: it was one of increasing disenchantment and disillusion.[53]

Within a month of his return, Klemperer was brooding over whether or not to join the Communist Party.

> I do not want to take a decision in accordance with my—vacillating— emotions, ... but coolly and calculatingly in accordance with what is best for *my* situation, *my* freedom, *the work I still have to do*, and yet *nevertheless serving my ideal task* [to prevent the return of Nazism], back the right horse. Which is the right horse? ... Russia? USA? Democracy? Communism? ... Unpolitical? Politically committed? Question mark upon question mark.

Four months later he took the plunge.

> The application forms for admission to the KPD [German Communist Party] are lying on my desk. Am I a coward if I do *not* join ...; am I a coward if I do join? Are my reasons for joining solely egotistical? No! ... It alone is really pressing for radical exclusion of the Nazis. But it replaces the old lack of freedom with a new one! But at the moment that is not to be avoided.

To become a member of the Communist Party, he concluded, was "a lesser evil." Klemperer was never convincing as a Marxist-Leninist; he was not a proper Communist, nor, for that matter, a proper Liberal, a proper German, or a proper Jew. Hence a repeated lament: "I am all the time sitting ... between stools."[54]

Paradoxically, Klemperer's sense of being perched, perilously so, enhanced his persuasiveness. A more confident and assured self-presentation would have belied the terror he was living through—and the desperate hope he placed in bearing witness.

Childhoods, Disrupted: Ruth Kluger and Michał Głowiński

Victor Klemperer could use his diary-writing to keep his emotional balance; he could use his professional training to analyze the linguistic practices of the Nazi regime. With it he conveyed a sense of strangeness: he depicted "a reality both absurd and ominous, a world altogether grotesque and chilling."[1] The protagonists of this chapter—Ruth Kluger, born 1931, and Michał Głowiński, born 1934—did not have Klemperer's intellectual tools at their disposal, at least not when they were living under Nazi rule. Years later they looked back on their childhoods; they summoned up untamed memories and sought to wrestle with them. For them, there is no forgetting the past, and there is no redemptive retelling of it.

These are not straightforward reckonings. Kluger and Głowiński keep interrupting their narratives to consider and reconsider the act of remembering. And in so doing, they project radically different images: in Kluger's work, there is a feisty, edgy, and angry figure calling up a child with the same sharp features; in Głowiński's text, there is a diffident subject evoking a terrified, dazed, numb youngster. These very different sensibilities, rather than analytical prowess, are central to what is on offer.

Both, by different means, put intense pressure on the reader. Will he or she—will we—be able to tolerate it? Will we be able to resist the temptation to invent a tidy ending?

"Timescapes"

In 1988 Kluger was serving as director of the University of California's Education Abroad Program in Göttingen. She had been in Germany only a few months when, crossing the street and in a pedestrian zone, a teenage bicyclist ran her down—not out of malice, she surmised. Everything turned black, and indeed she went in and out of consciousness for quite a while. Her thoughts "whirled in a circle or a spiral, formed the oddest geometrical figures, were never linear … Time was splintered." She didn't "experience it as a continuity but rather as a heap of broken glass, shards cutting into your mind when you try to put them together."[2] Within a few weeks she had recovered.

Yet "the memories remained, like cave paintings, which to the uninitiated eye at first seem mere scribbles, until they become figures and assume a spectral significance." At last, she sat down and wrote, in German—her mother tongue, but a language her mother refused to read. Kluger did not want her elderly parent to see this work; there was much in it about their tormented and tormenting relationship. The book, *weiter leben*, living on—appeared in 1992 and was a huge success. Her mother got wind of it, "found the passages critical of her, and was … hurt." She feared that her neighbors—who did not know German—would discover that she had been a bad mother. So Kluger decided to postpone issuing an English edition until after her mother's death. When she did publish *Still Alive: A Holocaust Childhood Remembered* in 2001, she made clear that it was "neither a translation nor a new book: it's another version, a parallel book if you will," for her children and an American audience.[3]

Kluger's first thought had been to call her book *Stations* and tie her diverse memories to the cities and camps she associated with them. (Then a Catholic friend reminded her of the stations of the cross. She "was appalled at the unintended hubris.") There should be, she wrote, "a word like *timescape* to indicate the nature of a place in time, that is, at a certain time, neither before nor after." The places she specified were not names of present or former homes: they were more like "piers of bridges that were blown up, only we can't be quite sure of what these bridges connected." And, she added, "if we don't find the bridges, we'll either have to invent them or content ourselves with living in a no-man's-land between past and present."[4]

* * *

"Their secret was death not sex." With this pithy statement, Kluger began her account. Eight-year-old Kluger was eavesdropping on the grown-ups' conversation. They were talking about Hans, a cousin, who had been in Buchenwald and had been tortured. The little girl wanted "to find out more about this extraordinary experience. Not so much from sympathy as from curiosity, because Hans was the center of an exciting mystery." Years later, visiting him—he had gotten out of Buchenwald, out of Austria, and had settled in England and married a non-Jew—Kluger had a chance to ask him "about the old secrets," and grabbed it. "But the other guests in the stifling space of the tidy English living room want to be left in peace: the children assure us that they were about to leave anyway and had better go now … Hans's gentile wife leaves the room. She has heard it all before and more than she wanted. True, no doubt, but did she ever pay attention?"[5] Will anyone pay attention to what Kluger has to tell?

"The grown-ups," Kluger wrote, recalling her childhood in Vienna, "had lost their bearings … My people knew of the pogroms of the past (they wouldn't have been Jews if they didn't), but these were dark, historical, preferably Polish and Russian matters—nothing to do with us. They also knew what had been going on in neighboring Germany for the past five years. Or didn't they read the newspapers? What *were* they thinking?" Kluger demanded "with self-righteous hindsight." After Hitler annexed Austria in March 1938, they should have gotten out, "legally or illegally, and regardless of destination. Just out. True they didn't have as much time as the German Jews to leave their country, but more than the Polish Jews." She would have left, she says, "with the feel of disaster still and forever" in her bones.[6]

The earliest disaster, Kluger's earliest loss—her brother, really her half-brother, Georg in German, Jiři in his native Czech. Her mother had had a son by her first husband. She had divorced him and returned to Vienna; her ex-husband remained in Prague. The boy had lived with his mother. "One day," Kluger had imagined, "I'd be like him, as far as a girl could. One day he was gone."[7] In 1938, after a summer vacation in Prague, he did not return. His father did not allow him to leave, and the Czech courts backed him up. Decades later, at dinner—Kluger was then teaching in Princeton's German department—a visiting lecturer, evidently Saul Friedländer, described in detail what had happened to a particular transport to Riga.[8] It had been her brother's transport.

Kluger lost her father as well. A gynecologist, he had been arrested on the charge of performing an illegal abortion. Thanks to Kluger's mother who mobilized and paid a well-placed and opportunistic lawyer, he was released on the condition that he leave the country and that his wife stay behind to pay "the infamous *Reichsfluchtsteuer*, literally a tax for flight from the Reich." Kluger recalled the scene of his homecoming—it ranked as an "incorrigible memory." "There was a big luncheon, lots of family and I had been allowed to bring my best friend to show her my newly released father. He was talking, and everyone was listening to him; he was the center of attention, and I wanted to be noticed by him, contact him … All it got me was a thrashing such as I had never had before, in front of my wide-eyed friend—the humiliation of it!—and being banished from the family table." A couple of days later he was gone, traveling first to Italy. "And there he made the mistake of fleeing from a fascist country to a democracy, to France. The Italians were much less prone to interfere with Jewish refugees than the French were, … for Italians have a healthy disrespect for government."[9] The French handed him over to the Germans, and in 1944 he was transported from Drancy. For years Kluger assumed that Auschwitz had been his final destination—and had imagined him in a cramped room full of people breathing in poison gas. Much, much later she learned that his transport ended up in Lithuania and Estonia. How he was murdered, she never did find out.

Vienna, Kluger quipped, "was a city that banished you and then didn't let you leave." "The Reich wanted to be compensated when its unwanted citizens actually left." Her mother explained: she couldn't find the money to pay the Reichsfluchtsteuer: "Jewish real estate had been confiscated and Jewish bank accounts couldn't be accessed by owners." Not satisfied, Kluger insisted reproachfully: "You had connections, you are pretty savvy, what happened to you?" (And Kluger wondered: could it have been her neuroses, her "cumulative madness, aggravated by the mad new social order?") Obliged to stay, the older woman refused to allow her daughter to leave.

Once when she and I were at the Jewish Community Center, a young man asked us whether she would consider sending me by myself with a children's transport to Palestine (or was it England? I'm not sure). It was a last chance, he said, just in the nick of time. Very advisable. My heart pounded, for I would dearly have loved to leave Vienna … She didn't ask me and didn't even look at me as she answered in an even voice: "No. A child and its mother belong together." On the way home I fought down my disappointment … Should she have asked my opinion? Not have treated me exclusively as her property? In her last years, when she was a broken old woman who had seen most of the century, with her faculties failing, I still now and then got a glimpse of this powerful claim to ownership, disguised as love and expressed as criticism. ("Why can't you visit me tomorrow?" "Do you *have* to travel?" "Where is your coat? It's too cold to go without." "You are wearing the wrong shoes.")[10]

Kluger and her mother were stuck in Vienna until September 1942. Five years earlier, that is, in the autumn of 1937, six months before the German invasion, Kluger had started first grade. Over the next four years, she attended eight different schools. Every day there were fewer and fewer students—the Jewish students had already been forced out of the state schools and sent to ones reserved for them. Kluger wondered: maybe the missing children had managed to leave the country; maybe they had gone underground; maybe they had been arrested. "When there were too few students, the school was closed," and Kluger "was transferred to another with the same problem ... The teachers, too, disappeared one after the other ... The fewer schools there were for Jewish children, the longer it took to get to school. You had to take the streetcars and the underground train. The longer it took, the less likely it was that one could avoid hateful glances and encounters." A vignette from this period:

> I have heard a Jewish woman about my age tell how she first experienced the Nazis. It was the sandbox, she said. She was playing in the sandbox, and one of the Aryan mothers simply threw her out. She thought at first it was a new game and promptly piled back in. The "game" was repeated. After the third time she understood. Jewish children are notoriously good learners. But what, I wonder, went on in the head of the woman who did this? And yet being thrown out of our sandbox for no apparent reason by the parents of other kids—that was the quintessential experience of my generation of preschoolers and first graders in Hitler's Vienna.[11]

Changing schools—until her mother suggested that she stop going to school altogether; changing house—until she and her mother were transported to Theresienstadt. The first two homes, Kluger recalled, "were bright and sunny." The next two were dismal: dark apartments that they shared with a couple of other Jewish families. She and her mother "had a small room, which got its only light from an inner courtyard ... There were bedbugs. You turn out the light and imagine the bugs crawling out of the mattress. Then you get bitten and turn on the light and complain bitterly that the repulsive vermin are sharing your bed." Still, her mother tried to remain in Vienna as long as possible—it helped that she had a job as a nurse and physical therapist at the Jewish hospital. (Kluger often spent her days at the hospital alone with a book. At least there she could get a meal and take a shower.) The two of them were "among the last Jews to be deported from Vienna to Theresienstadt, in the so-called hospital transport of September 1942."[12]

Kluger's obvious hostility toward her mother—her memoir is peppered with moments of sheer ingratitude—is all the more unsettling in the context of Hitler's genocidal project. It makes havoc of one's assumption that, somehow, the absolute horror of the persecution would have done away with family dramas.

* * *

"Theresienstadt wasn't all that bad," so the German wife of a Princeton colleague informed Kluger—with more than a hint of smugness. This woman, whom Kluger called Gisela, belonged "to a younger generation of Germans who couldn't be blamed for anything ... She was determined to reduce the past until it fit into the box of a clean German conscience that won't cause her countrymen to lose any sleep. Some Germans, it would seem, are caught up in a kind of ... melodrama, where the nuances of reality and its gritty surfaces disappear in a fog, and you can't make out any details, so why try?" Ditto most Americans. Gisela's remark was "a provocation and unmistakably aggressive."[13]

Theresienstadt had been built in the 1780s. This small fortified town had served as a minor military base for the Hapsburg Monarchy until 1918 and then for the Czechoslovak Republic. In September 1938, at the Munich Conference, Britain, France, Italy, and Germany—the Czechs had been banished to the wings—had agreed that the Sudetenland should become part of the German Reich. Thereseinstadt remained in the rump Czecho-Slovak state—the newly introduced hyphen stemmed from a Slovak demand. Six months later, the Wehrmacht occupied Prague, and Czecho-Slovakia ceased to exist. Slovakia became a German satellite; Bohemia-Moravia was turned into a protectorate of the Reich. And Theresienstadt fell under German control. By the autumn of 1941, it housed some 7,000 German soldiers and Czech civilians, and an annex served as the central Gestapo prison in the Protectorate. At the end of the year, Jewish labor details converted it for its new function, a transit camp/

ghetto—as Kluger put it, "the stable that supported the slaughterhouse."[14] Czech, German, and Austrian Jews were shipped from Theresienstadt to killing centers, concentration camps, and forced labor camps in German-occupied Poland, Belorussia (now Belarus), and the Baltic States. In addition, Theresienstadt served as a "retirement" community for the elderly or disabled Jews of Germany and Austria as well as highly decorated war veterans. It was expected that the conditions within the camp would hasten the death of many, mostly from disease or starvation. Of the roughly 140,000 Jews transferred to Theresienstadt, nearly 90,000 were deported to points further east and almost certain death, and approximately 30,000 died in Theresienstadt itself.

"Life in a big stable. The owners occasionally show up in their ominous uniforms to make sure the cattle behave"—that was Theresienstadt, so overpopulated that it was "almost impossible to find a quiet spot for a private conversation ... No freedom of movement beyond a square kilometer, and within the camp you were at the mercy of an anonymous will, which could, and would, send you to some vaguely perceived but frightening destination ... That was the framework of our existence, this coming and going of Jews who could make no decisions, had no influence on what was decided for them, and didn't know when and how a decision regarding them would be made." So Kluger hated this "mudhole," this "cesspool," this "ant heap."[15]

But she also loved it. Vienna had treated her like an "outcast." It had made her into "an eccentric oddball of a child." She was used to the company of hospital patients, nurses, and the grown-ups with whom she shared an apartment; she was used to amusing herself "mostly with books, and mostly with adult books at that." In Theresienstadt she was assigned to L414, a room for the youngest group of girls—thirty girls in a space that would have been comfortable for two or three. At first, when her mother came to visit, Kluger begged to go off with her. Her mother refused, leaving Kluger to cope as best she could. And she coped well. As she saw it: "At bottom I wasn't too unhappy to escape from my mother's contradictory demands, and it soon dawned on me that it might be easier to live with other kids. I observed the behavior of the girls around me and saw that it wouldn't be too hard to please them. In the end I developed a gift for friendship."[16]

"Regular instruction for the children of Theresienstadt was illegal." Kluger did have irregular instruction. There were plenty of teachers: Theresienstadt was "brimful of men and women of the Jewish intelligentsia, ... happy if some children sat at their feet and listened to them talk about Culture (with a capital C of course)." Kluger recalled hearing the famous Berlin rabbi, Leo Baeck; he spoke to her group of the Bible and the Enlightenment and told them they could have both, the old myth and the new science. And she recalled her introduction to Zionism. The administration of L414 was in the hands of a sixteen-year-old who turned her community into a youth movement: they sang Zionist songs and danced the hora; when they went to bed, they "didn't wish each other *Gute Nacht*, but *leila tov*." Years later, Kluger wondered how she, an unbeliever, could call herself a Jew: "It's because of Theresienstadt. That is where I became a Jew."[17]

Was Gisela right—that Theresienstadt hadn't been all that bad? Kluger interjected, "where did she get off lecturing me on this place from my past, where everything that came from the Germans was pure malice and the good had its only source in us, the prisoners?"[18]

* * *

"I used to think," Kluger wrote, "that after the war I would have something of significance and interest to tell. A contribution. But people didn't want to hear about it."[19] She rarely had a chance to talk about events that ranked as unforgettable—like the transport to Auschwitz in May 1944.

The distance from Theresienstadt to Auschwitz—as the crow flies—is not great; in an overcrowded cattle car, it was very long indeed. "The train stood around, the temperature rose ... A whiff of panic trembled in the air."

> An old woman who sat next to my mother gradually fell apart: first she cried and whimpered, and I grew impatient and angry with her, because here she was adding her private disintegration to the great evil of our collective helplessness. A defense reaction: I could not face or assimilate the reality of a grown-up losing her mind before my eyes. Finally this woman pushed herself onto my mother's lap and urinated. I still see the tense look of revulsion on my mother's face in the slanting twilight of the car, and how she gently pushed the woman from her lap. Not brutally and without malice ... It was a pragmatic, humane gesture, like a nurse might employ to free herself from a clinging patient. I thought my mother should have been indignant, but for her the situation was beyond anger and outrage.[20]

Birkenau—their destination—was the extermination camp of Auschwitz. Kluger and her mother were herded to subdivision B2B, the so-called family camp. Established in September 1943 with the arrival of 5,000 Jews from Theresienstadt, the camp was unusual in a number of respects: men, women, and children were housed together; they did not undergo the standard selection process, that is, separating those fit for labor, who were allowed to live until they were worked to death, from those deemed unfit, who were liquidated straightaway; they kept their civilian clothes; and their heads were not shaved. In December 1943 that first transport was joined by a second, again from Theresienstadt carrying 5,000 additional Jews, and then in May 1944 another two transports arrived. All these deportees lived under the same harsh conditions—conditions that produced an extremely high rate of "natural" deaths. Yet "except for the position of ... [senior camp inmate], which was filled by a veteran German criminal ..., the internal administration of the camp was in the hands of the Jews."[21] (Why this special status? Most likely the Nazis wanted to use the family camp as a propaganda showcase in the event of a visit by the International Committee of the Red Cross—a visit that never happened.[22])

Whatever its purpose, six months to the day after entering the camp, all those who had come in September 1943 were exterminated—in one fell swoop, with no selections being made. Not so the final liquidation in July 1944. Now there was to be a selection. "At a certain barracks at a certain time, women between the ages of fifteen and forty-five were to be chosen for a transport to a labor camp." Kluger's mother believed, quite rightly, "that Birkenau was the pits, and to get out was better than to stay. But the word *Selektion* was not a good word in Auschwitz, because it usually meant the gas chambers."

> Two SS men conducted the selection, both with their backs to the rear wall [of the barrack]. They stood on opposite sides of the so-called chimney, which divided the room. In front of each was a line of naked, or almost naked, women, waiting to be judged. The selector in whose line I stood had a round, wicked mask of a face and was so tall that I had to crane my neck to look up to him. I told him my age, and he turned me down with a shake of his head, simply like that. Next to him, the woman clerk, a prisoner, too, was not to write down my number ... My mother had been chosen. No wonder: she was the right age, a grown-up woman. We stood on the street between ... two rows of barracks and argued.[23]

Kluger's mother pleaded with her daughter to try again. She urged Kluger to sneak into the barrack by way of the back door—the day was hot, and both the front and back doors were open—and get into the other line, this time telling the SS man that she was fifteen, thus adding three years to her age. Kluger remonstrated: "I don't look older." Back and forth they went. Half desperately, half contemptuously, the mother said: "'You are a coward,' ... and added 'I wasn't ever a coward.'" Kluger reluctantly agreed to try, with the proviso that she would say she was thirteen. "Fifteen was preposterous." Without being noticed, she managed to go in by the back door, slink around to the front, take off her clothes once more, and quietly move to the end of the line. She had proved to her mother that she wasn't a chicken. But she "was the smallest, and obviously the youngest, female around, undeveloped, undernourished, and nowhere near puberty."

> The line moved towards an SS man who, unlike the first, was in a good mood ... His clerk was perhaps nineteen or twenty. When she saw me, she left her post, and almost within the hearing of her boss, she asked me quickly and quietly and with an unforgettable smile of her irregular teeth: "How old are you?" "Thirteen," I said, as planned. Fixing me intently, she whispered, "Tell him you are fifteen."
>
> Two minutes later it was my turn ... When asked for my age I gave the decisive answer, which I had scorned when my mother suggested it but accepted from the stranger. "I am fifteen."
>
> "She seems small," the master of life and death remarked. He sounded almost friendly, as if he was evaluating cows and calves.
>
> "But she is strong," the woman said, "look at the muscles in her legs. She can work."
>
> She didn't know me, so why did she do it? He agreed—why not? She made a note of my number, and I had won an extension on life.[24]

The girl was herself an inmate, and she risked a great deal when she prompted Kluger to lie and then openly championed someone "too young and small for forced labor ... She saw me stand in line," Kluger wrote, "she defended me, and she got me through." The girl's act, she insisted, was "of the kind that is always unique, no matter how often it occurs: an incomprehensible act of grace, or put more modestly, a good deed."[25]

* * *

Again a trip in a freight car; but this time not too many women for the space. The train took them to Christianstadt, a satellite camp of Gross-Rosen.

There they lived in barracks, which, unlike the large stable-like structures in Birkenau, had real rooms, with six to twelve persons per room. At first, Kluger's contingent of Czechs, Germans, Austrians, and Hungarians from the Theresienstadt family camp were the only prisoners. "Then some Eastern European Jews arrived who spoke Yiddish and had been selected directly from the ramp in Auschwitz." Right away there was a caste system, until the social distinctions were trumped by economics: by the difference between the cooks and their children who grew fat—"actually fat"—and the rest who had so little to eat that all they could think about was food.[26]

A day went something like this. Awakened by a siren, then standing in rows of five for roll call. A "black, coffeelike brew for breakfast, a ration of bread to take along, and marched off in rows of three." (A guard ran alongside the women, whistling to make them keep step. No use. "Try to teach Jewish housewives— that's what most of them were, of course—to act like army recruits.") Then to work: heavy labor, clearing forests, excavating, carrying tree trunks, laying out railroad lines. Sometimes Kluger was lent out to nearby villagers: it meant work indoors, out of the bitter, winter cold. Sometimes she had to work in the quarry—that was the worst: clothes too thin, feet wrapped in newspapers, longing for time to pass. At night the older women talked about their prewar lives—travel, parties, university studies, and cooking. They exchanged recipes, listing generous amounts of butter, eggs, and sugar—a fantasy baking contest. Kluger "listened with a growling stomach."[27]

Once, when working in the forest—there the prisoners had contact with German civilians—Kluger sat down, during a rest period, on a tree trunk next to "a fat, squarish man." He must have invited her to join him; she never would have done so on her own accord. "He was eating a sandwich of lard on rye, a delicacy not to be found in the camp," and she wondered how she could get him to give it to her. He was obviously curious about her, "a dark-haired … child prisoner, … unsuited for the work, … a girl at that, who spoke flawless and presumably native German, … a kid who belonged in school." He asked a series of questions; she answered with reserve and with an eye on the sandwich—she didn't get his bread and lard, though he did cut off a large bite for her. The civilian, for his part, told her "that German children, too, didn't go to school anymore. They had gone to soldier, everyone." Kluger summed up:

I imagine that in the mind of the fat man, if he is still around, I am a little Jewish girl who wasn't all that badly off, for she didn't tell any horror stories, though he encouraged her in a friendly way to be honest and chat about her life ... And perhaps he uses this encounter as evidence that Jews were no worse off during the war than the rest of the population.[28]

* * *

Nazi records show that at the start of 1945 "there were some seven hundred and fourteen thousand prisoners in the concentration camp network." (One can assume that the actual numbers were much higher: even those in charge "were unable to gauge its vast dimensions with absolute accuracy.") The prisoners were "dispersed in hundreds of camps, large and small, over the length and breadth of the disintegrating Nazi empire, from the Rhine in the west ... to the Vistula in the east, from the Baltic shore in the north to the Danube in the south." Hundreds of thousands of them "were forced-marched ... through the length and breadth of the collapsing Third Reich." Those marches proved lethal: prisoners "were gradually liquidated, whether before departure, during the march, or after arriving at their destinations." In early May, when Germany finally capitulated, perhaps 250,000 were dead and many others, because of their desperate physical condition, did not survive long after liberation.[29]

Christianstadt was among the camps evacuated ahead of the advancing Russians. On the second night of the trek—the women were now on foot— Kluger, her mother, and Susi, a girl slightly older than Kluger whom her mother had adopted in Birkenau, made their escape. (The most "unusual thing" Kluger could say about her parent was this: "she adopted a child in Birkenau"; she simply decreed that Susi belonged with them.) As the freezing, hungry prisoners were waiting for the SS to commandeer a barn in which they could sleep, the three of them ran away. It was their luck, Kluger wrote, "to be caught up in the general dismemberment of the old Germany," and they "followed ... the newly homeless who were choking on their own misery and hadn't the stomach" to investigate where they came from.[30] They begged and stole—both were relatively easy. They managed to get secondhand clothing and look less suspicious, and they managed to get enough to eat. Soon, like the refugees, they were heading west.

They needed identification: they needed proof that they were indeed a family. Kluger's mother insisted that she would take care of it. How? Her strategy: go to a village pastor, tell their tale, and ask for help. (The girls were skeptical: in their short lives, they "had not seen many examples of Christian love for neighbor or for enemy.") It worked. Kluger's mother reported "that the pastor had been practically speechless and didn't hesitate for a moment. He didn't consider whether he was breaking the law, but rushed to his files and feverishly started to look for the right thing. He had baptismal certificates and other documents that were deposited in churches, and gave" her "papers for a mother and two daughters. There were some improbabilities, like imperfect dates of birth."[31] Still, the papers were a godsend.

That night the three of them boarded a train headed to southern Germany. They had to decide quickly because trains were infrequent, and one couldn't be sure when there would be another. The train was also slow, often stopping in order to avoid bombers—this was the period of the last and heaviest air attacks. So the train crawled along for days, landing Kluger and her companions in Straubing, in lower Bavaria. There they were treated as fellow citizens, assigned a place to stay, and lodged on a small farm at the edge of town. And there they were when the "Amis," the Americans, arrived.

> We hadn't planned any further than this moment. The three of us walked to the center of town, looked at each other in amazement, and asked: "What now?" My mother, determined to try out her English, walked up to the first American uniform in view, a military policeman directing traffic, and told him in a few words that we had escaped from a concentration camp. Since I knew no English, I couldn't understand his answer, but his gesture was unmistakable. He put his hands over his ears and turned away. My mother translated. He had had his fill of people who had claimed they had been in the camps. They were all over the place. Please, leave him alone![32]

* * *

Mother's knowledge of English stood them in good stead: she was "hired as an assistant and interpreter to a Jewish officer and helped with the DPs, or displaced persons," people like themselves, "who had escaped or been liberated or come out of hiding. They either wanted to get back home or to emigrate."[33] The three of them made their way to the United States, Susi to St. Louis, thanks to the efforts of an uncle, Kluger and her mother to New York in late 1947.

At their first Thanksgiving, spent at the home of distant relatives, who "had lived on Long Island forever," the hostess lectured Kluger: "'You have to erase from your memory everything that happened in Europe. You have to make a new beginning. You have to forget what they did to you. Wipe it off like chalk from a blackboard.' And to make me understand better, she gestured as if wiping a board with a sponge ... Struggling with foreign words ..., I told her why I had to reject this invitation to betray my people, my dead. The language was recalcitrant." The older woman "hardly listened to my alien gibberish."[34]

Once again Kluger wove together her Holocaust story and her ongoing struggle to find an audience that is both curious and sympathetic. A friend commented on her quest: "You complain that no one asked questions. But you also complain about the questions they did ask. You are hard to satisfy." Kluger concurred: "Damn right, I *am* hard to satisfy."[35]

"Flashes of memory"

Michał Głowiński, a professor literature and a literary critic, had established a reputation with theoretical studies of the novel before turning to autobiography. *Czarne sezony* came out in Poland in 1998 to great acclaim; seven years later it appeared in English as *The Black Seasons*, translated by Marci Shore. The book is not a simple chronological account of the war years; it is not a continuous record of life under the German occupation. Głowiński did not aim to reconstruct that bleak history; what he aimed to do was to capture his experiences, experiences "emerging from flashes of memory," to tell of "events only in the form" in which he "perceived them at the time." He warned his reader: "Flashes of memory ... justify fragmentariness—indeed, they assume this from the outset."[36] Just the barest hint of what was to follow.

* * *

Głowiński began with a word: ghetto. "I remember when I heard it for the first time," shortly before his fifth birthday, right after the defeat in September 1939. "The word drifted into my ears as people around me deliberated ... I envisioned this mysterious and incomprehensible ghetto as a huge, many-storied carriage riding through the streets of the city, pulled by some umpteen horses ... I imagined that in this carriage there would be all kinds of staircases ... and many windows as well ... In my imagination, I conjured up this fantastical carriage on the model of a hearse—the black carriage of death—such as could be seen from time to time in our city."[37]

The first ghetto in the General Government was created at Radomsko in December 1939. (Large chunks of Poland had been annexed to the Third Reich. The rest of German-occupied Poland, known as the General Government, included the Lublin district and parts of the provinces of Warsaw and Kraków.) In May 1940, Hans Frank, the governor general, ordered that the Jews of Warsaw be corralled into an exclusively Jewish area of the city. In November, that area was sealed off. Having lived through the siege of Warsaw in the very center of the city, having then been confined, along with other members of his culturally assimilated family, to a small ghetto in Pruszków, and finally having been relocated to the Warsaw ghetto—"a trip in a sealed railway car [that] lasted two days," even though the distance traveled was "just over a dozen kilometers"—Głowiński quickly learned the real meaning of the word that had inspired such delightful fancies.[38]

The color, "a gray-brown-black, the only one of its kind, devoid of any brighter ... [hue] or distinguishing accent": this monochromatism, this "discoloredness" characterized the ghetto. Głowiński recalled: "Everything was just that—discolored—regardless of what its original color had been and irrespective of the weather. Even the most intensive rays of sunlight would not brighten or even vaguely tint this discoloredness." In his mind's eye, "the color of the ghetto" was "the color of the paper that covered the corpses lying in the street before they were taken away"—the paper itself became for him "one of death's embodiments." And in the "season of the great dying," which "lasted without interruption in the ghetto, ... corpses belonged to the permanent landscape ... The street was a place of death: not only sudden and unexpected death, but also slow death—from hunger, from disease, and from every other possible cause."[39]

A memory: "a skeleton, clothed in an overcoat, playing the violin." As Głowiński walked to lessons—only briefly did he have an opportunity for any schooling—he passed "an emaciated man, no longer young, playing the violin. He always played the same tune," which Głowiński learned from an adult was "a fragment of Mendelssohn's Violin Concerto. It was said that before the war the violinist had been member of the Warsaw Philharmonic Orchestra ... There was so little of him that he faded away into his wide gray overcoat, which undoubtedly had fit him during better prewar times, but which now hung on him as if made for three such men as him ... He must have succeeded in collecting something, but ... destitution and hunger were ever more visible in his appearance."[40]

Another memory: a "scarecrow," a "tall, very thin man, slightly hunchbacked, whose movements ... seemed mechanical." He gave the impression of having been "artificially put together from different parts: his head, with oddly protruding cheeks and wire glasses falling down his nose," looked as if it has "been fastened with screws into the rest of his body." Głowiński saw him from time to time when he went to class. This strange-looking fellow occupied the same apartment as his teacher. Knocking on the door one day, the boy was told that the apartment mate had just hanged himself. "The image of that dead man dangling in the bathroom haunted" Głowiński for a long time. It was then, he surmised, that he "grasped what death was."[41]

* * *

Starting in July 1942, as part of Operation Reinhard—the code name for the German plan to murder the approximately two million Jews living in the General Government—Jews from the Warsaw ghetto were packed off to Treblinka and exterminated, all told approximately 300,000. Word came that Głowiński and his parents were to be rounded up and marched to the collection point—the Umschlagplatz—created by fencing off a part of a freight train station. Instead they and a number of neighbors hid in a cellar. "It was crowded, and the vault so low that it was impossible to stand ... Every sound from outside brought terror ... I, too," Głowiński wrote, "was overcome with fear. I nestled close to my parents, though in such a situation, even they were no guarantee of safety—I realized that they were threatened by the same thing as I was, as we all were. It was dark, absolute silence was obligatory, no sign of life was permitted to escape from behind those walls."[42]

How, then, did Głowiński and his parents manage to survive? He confessed himself to be "astonished, ... astonished by all of it," astonished to be alive. He recalled being herded to the Umschlagplatz; he recalled being "pushed and dragged through the streets by the Germans and their Ukrainian and Lithuanian-Latvian accessories as well as by Jewish policemen." When he and his parents reached the collection point, "the freight cars were already waiting, the train was preparing to set off. That day the Germans had taken more people than they could transport, and some would have to stay behind," including the three of them. Those remaining "settled temporarily in spots on the ground, each one … thinking how to get out." By chance, Głowiński's father "met someone he had known in his youth, someone he hadn't seen in years and who was now a Jewish policeman." He asked for help, and the man led them to "a dark place, something resembling a packing room or a narrow corridor where … household goods must have once been stored." They were "to stay there until the German divisions, having completed their tasks for the day, left the ghetto. And so it happened." The acquaintance led them out of the "Umschlagplatz via a side exit, perhaps through a hole in the fence."[43]

The three of them escaped the ghetto itself—and thus "succeeded in evading annihilation" in January 1943. Finding someone to get them across the boundary was no simple matter. Głowiński recalled that his father arranged this with a man, no longer young, by the name of Kryształ. During the "final phase in the ghetto, Kryształ performed some function, he must have been an official in contact with the Germans … He knew a German soldier … who was willing, under certain conditions and for a price, to transport Jews across the ghetto's borders. He insisted [that] they not have a Semitic appearance, and … he charged Kryształ with making that judgment." Kryształ appraised the parents at their place of work, "where the only kind of work was slave labor"; it remained for him to see what the boy looked like.[44] Now, for the first time in several months, Głowiński ventured out of the apartment. Kryształ rendered a favorable verdict, and the German soldier agreed to convey the boy and his parents.

They got out in a "luxurious" way—unlike some of his relatives, they did not cross to the other side in the sewer canals. They got out in a car driven by the German soldier. In settling on a date, the soldier had to know "who would be standing guard that day," who, "even if not eager to allow anyone to get out," would be "sufficiently indifferent and uninquisitive" so as not to notice the three of them crouched in the back seat, dressed as inconspicuously as possible. The stop at the exit was brief: the soldier presented his documents, and they were quickly on their way. Głowiński and his parents thus "found themselves on the Aryan side."[45]

* * *

They were not safe. Głowiński, his mother, and an aunt—his father was hiding out elsewhere in Warsaw—were concealed in an attic. The space was empty and in lamentable condition: the walls were stained with mildew, the electricity had been shut off, and there was no heat—"only a ... cast-iron stove with a long pipe, which served as an oven ... There was no furniture save two stools"—the three of them slept on straw-filled mattresses.[46]

The boy was playing chess by himself and against himself—in the ghetto he had had a chess set and a book describing the matches played by the great chess masters, in the attic he still had the same wooden pieces and a bedraggled chess board, but no book—when someone knocked, imperiously, on the door. It was not the caretaker. It was a stranger, "a young man dressed elegantly in accordance with occupation-era fashion." The stranger declared he knew who they were and that he would hand them over to the Germans—unless he were bribed to keep quiet. They had neither money nor valuables. Głowiński's father, however, possessed both "a little money and the remaining jewelry, set aside for a black hour ... At the end of long negotiations, it was decided that ... [the aunt]" would contact the father and return with the ransom.[47] In the meantime Głowiński and his mother would remain in the attic as hostages.

Silence. Prolonged waiting. The blackmailer sat calmly on one of the stools. Głowiński sat vacantly on a mattress, the chessboard laid out in front of him. In no "state to play in a sensible manner," he moved the pieces around without rhyme or reason. "At a certain moment ... the bored *szmalcownik* [blackmailer]" proposed that the two of them play a game. The "chess match ... against the *szmalcownik*—or rather, against Death, who on this occasion had assumed the form not of a skeleton with a scythe, but rather of a well-built man with a roguishly trimmed moustache"—was never finished.[48] The aunt returned.

Following the szmalcownik's departure—he left sulky and discontented with what he had extracted—it was obvious that the threesome could not remain in the attic. "The location was now exposed, or as people said then 'burnt.'" They could not "naively presume that the szmalcownik would not return," nor could they "dismiss the possibility that he would send along a friend and the whole scene would begin anew." It was too close to curfew for them to leave immediately. The next day, as the curfew ended, they set out. Mother and aunt took some small bundles; Głowiński took his chess set. "A new stage of flight from death began."[49]

* * *

A bleak day in December 1943. For much of the year Głowiński and his mother had taken cover in a village. Now that had grown too dangerous, and they had returned to Warsaw. For a short time they stayed with people named Bobrowski—people who made a business out of harboring Jews and charging steep fees. It was a temporary solution, and mother was trying to find a longer-term hiding place. "Procuring even the worst room for a Jewish woman with a child was, understandably, a nontrivial task. But this finally was achieved. A place was found!" They were "to be settled in the basement of an inhabited though unfinished villa."[50] They were to appear at an agreed-upon time, just after the curfew ended.

And so they ventured forth. That basement in the villa "became a tremendous prospect, even though there was, of course, no guarantee that it was a secure refuge." When they reached their destination, having moved through the streets in such a way as not to be noticed, they saw "something that completely stunned" them: a villa destroyed by fire—"a villa just after a fire had been put out, an ordinary, natural fire having nothing to do with the war and the occupation, a fire that might have broken out in peaceful and untroubled times. The fire brigade had only just left."[51]

Where were they to go? Making contact with family in Warsaw had already proved difficult; there was no way to communicate with Polish friends who had been helping; and father was now in Kielce, employed as a laborer, with an assumed, non-Jewish identity. For several hours they hid in the basement—until the owner came to warn and instruct them. They had been spotted and they must leave forthwith. They made their way back to the Bobrowskis, rang the doorbell and pleaded: "being left on the streets just before curfew was an unambiguous death sentence." Pani Bobrowski grudgingly let them in. "The events of that awful day had come full circle."[52]

The mother stayed only a couple of days; the boy remained about a week. Głowiński now had to part with his mother for the first time—and the separation lasted until the end of the war. It "came as a terrible shock."[53]

* * *

There was a desperate search for a place for even a couple of nights for the boy. It fell to another aunt, Maria, his mother's younger sister to deal with this "very problematic situation ... Among all the family members in hiding ... she moved about the Aryan side most freely. She possessed what were then called "'good looks,' which were not merely a privilege, but ... a divine bestowal ... People with good looks did not draw attention, they could blend into the crowd, it was easier for them to play the role of someone they were not. Maria's looks were exquisite; she was an attractive blond who looked as if she had been born into a noble estate, rather than into a Jewish merchant's family."[54]

Głowiński could not trace the chronology of his "miserable roamings" on the Aryan side, but he did recall—vividly—a short episode, an episode that lasted no more than a quarter of an hour and that took place somewhere in downtown Warsaw. Maria had to make a phone call. The two of them "entered a small pastry shop, where she thought there was a telephone ... There was not." So she decided to leave the boy alone for a few minutes. She bought him a pastry, ushered him to the least visible table in a dark corner, and told him "she would be ... back as soon as she had made the phone call." She told the same thing to the woman who had served them, who must have been the shop owner. There were no more than five tables and very few people. The boy sat quietly, like a mouse—and "nothing was happening." He ate his pastry. The women were chatting among themselves. But after a few minutes, he realized that he was being closely watched:

> The women—perhaps shop assistants, perhaps customers—had gathered around the shop owner, whispering and observing me intently ... Fragments of their conversation reached me ... I heard "A Jew, there's no question, a Jew." "She certainly isn't, but him—he's a Jew." "She foisted him off on us." The women deliberated: what should they do with me? The shop owner opened the door leading to the back room where the oven must have been, and called out "Hela! Hela, come look." And after some time Hela appeared in a flour-covered apron ... Perhaps she was ... an expert in racial questions ... One more pair of piercing eyes came forward to examine me.

Their curiosity, now piqued, the women approached the table where the boy sat—and began their interrogation.

> First one of them asked my name. I had false papers, I'd learned my identity, and I answered politely. Another ... [wanted to know] about my relationship with the woman who'd brought me there. I answered again, this time truthfully ... They continued to inundate me with questions. What were my parents doing? Where was I from? Where had I recently been? Where was I going? ... and so forth ... By then I'd ceased to answer, only from time to

time muttering a "yes" or "no." ... I heard not only the questions directed at me, but also the comments the women expressed ... to the side, as if only to themselves, but in such a way that I couldn't fail to hear ... Most often they spit out the threatening word "Jew," ... [and] also most terrifyingly, they kept repeating, "We must let the police know."

After about fifteen minutes, Maria returned. She had had trouble finding a telephone and had been gone longer that she had anticipated. When she saw the women gathered around the table, "she understood at once what was going on."[55]

In retrospect, Głowiński surmised that the women were not "driven by pure hatred or resentment; rather, they dreaded the problem that had suddenly fallen into their laps and were prepared to do anything—by whatever means and at whatever price—to rid themselves of it as quickly as possible."[56] Ridding themselves of the problem meant ridding themselves of the boy.

* * *

In early 1944, Głowiński found refuge in a convent in Turkowice. Several decades later he learned that the nuns "had hidden and rescued over thirty Jewish children—a very large, improbably large, number, every seventh or eighth child there was marked by origins that, if revealed, equated to a death sentence."[57] The convent was secluded, located close to Poland's eastern frontier. Left to its own devices, it offered no protection against German troops or Ukrainian partisans. At the center of this almost hermetically sealed world stood the chapel. Naturally it was the most important place for the nuns, but it was also the most important place for the convent's wards, Głowiński among them. He often went there, finding what otherwise eluded him—some peace and tranquility.

On a Sunday morning in July, the boy was alone after mass: the other children had scattered, some taking off for the nearby river, others heading for the woods. Głowiński, afraid to venture any distance from the convent, was circling a space behind the boys' house that had once been a garden, but was now a "chaos of untended plants." All of a sudden, the three brothers Z. appeared on the scene. Głowiński knew them, though he had not had personal contact with them. Evidently, he reasoned, they too had decided to stay behind after mass. The brothers were almost always seen together; the youngest was Głowiński's age—roughly ten—and the eldest was five years older. "This fifteen-year-old was clearly the leader of the family, while the younger brothers submitted unquestionably to him, playing the roles he assigned them." What those roles were, Głowiński soon learned:

> They surrounded me as if they wanted to form a snare and render impossible my escape … I didn't know what was going on or what they could want from me. I'd never gotten in their way … The eldest spoke up …: "We know you're a Jew. The Germans will be here tomorrow. We'll tell them, and they'll put you in your place."

Of course, Głowiński reflected, after so many years, he could not be sure of the precise words; nevertheless, the meaning had "imprinted itself deeply" on his memory.[58]

Face to face with the brothers Z., Głowiński stood absolutely still—paralyzed by fear, motionless, as if rooted to the spot. (For years he had hoped to find a description of the fear he then experienced, but to no avail. "Fear … arising from the most basic threats," he concluded, "defies description.") "Persuading them that this was nonsense, that I wasn't a Jew, would have been futile, it could only have irritated and provoked them. Nor would it have made sense to plead with them not to do that, that it would end badly for me and after all, I had done nothing to them. It would have … constituted an admission, and … an admission could only confirm the brothers Z. in their zealous intent … I was young, a child, yet accidents of fate had already instilled in me the wisdom of remaining silent when speaking was not an absolute necessity."[59]

What struck Głowiński most was the news that the Germans would arrive the next day. What should he do? Should he "submit passively to fate?" Should be run away? Finally he began to "search … feverishly" for Sister Róża, the preceptress of his group. From his flustered state, she guessed that he had something urgent to say. But not in the hallway. They went together to a place called the storage room. ("The name was a matter of custom, since the household objects that would … [have been] stored there were lacking.") Głowiński unburdened himself, and Sister Róża told him not to worry: "no one had said anything about Germans coming to Turkowice," and even if they did, the borthers Z. would not dare to do what they had threatened. In the end, something surprising happened:

> Sister Róża took from the cupboard a slice of bread, smeared it with butter
> (I noticed the remainder was kept in a small clay pot), and handed it to

me, saying that I should eat it here, at once. There was no need for more
prodding; at that time there was ever greater hunger in the convent, bread
was rigidly apportioned and had become the object of incessant desire, and
butter had become something entirely unfamiliar, perhaps its existence had
been forgotten. That chunk of wholemeal bread … was something more than
a piece of food satisfying hunger—it transformed itself into a sign imparting
to me that there were people here who were kind to me … Naturally … I …
could not be entirely convinced that … [the brothers Z.] would not do what
they had threatened if the Germans were actually to invade our convent.[60]

Nothing of the sort occurred: the Germans did not come the following day;
they never again appeared in Turkowice.

Not long thereafter "the first echoes of the front, detonations and
repeated gunshots" could be heard in the distance. "The Red Army entered
Turkowice without a battle, a division pitched its tents on nearby fields that
were lying fallow." For several days the soldiers moved about the area; "they
were dirty and … exhausted, and they rolled cigarettes from shag tobacco
and scraps of old newspapers." The nuns had expected the worst: "they
knew how the Bolsheviks had treated the clergy during the revolution,"
but nothing at all happened to confirm their fears. As for Głowiński, he
portrayed himself as still so "intimidated and stupefied" that he failed to
appreciate the significance of the events.[61] He recalled no sense of triumph
that he had survived the war.

* * *

When Głowiński arrived at the convent, he had already had two brief stays in
religious boarding schools and had a superficial acquaintance with Catholicism.
The roughly eighteen months in Turkowice was the one period in his life that
he was a "believer, deeply devout," enchanted by the rituals and observances,
enchanted by the hymns and religious pictures. Once he returned home, "faith
disappeared as quickly as it had come." Years later, he reflected on the "sudden
piety." During the occupation it could not bring someone such as himself a
feeling of safety, yet "the image of a protective and just God made it possible to
… take consolation from the fact that this sinister and abominable world was
not the only one." And he dreamt that he, too, "would be an acolyte," like some
of his classmates, and thereby have "more direct contact with God."[62] This did
not happen, even after his baptism.

Not until he had been in Turkowice for more than a year—and his mother had had a chance to give her permission—did the ceremony take place. No special lessons preceded it. None was necessary: for reasons of safety, the Mother Superior had decided that the Jewish children "would be allowed to take part in all religious practices and … would be treated like all the other children who had belonged to the Catholic Church since birth." The act itself took place on a sunny afternoon in the priest's chamber, "not merely without publicity, but in secret." Sister Róża took him to the so-called storage room in order for him to change from his ragged everyday clothes into something more appropriate, actually a threadbare outfit reminiscent of the 1920s. After the rite, he came back to the storage room, unseen, and returned the ceremonial attire. By then, that is, the spring of 1945, "the exposure of the fact" that Głowiński was a "Jew who had … received baptism and become a Catholic … only in Turkowice, no longer brought the threat of death."[63] Even so had his classmates learned of it, they would have pointed fingers and embittered his life.

* * *

Głowiński's mother had appeared in Turkowice a few months earlier, on a "cold and dismal day in February." He was sitting, as usual, "passive and unreflective, on a hard wooden bench"—"busy doing nothing and thinking about nothing." One of the boys came into the room and called out: "Your mother's come."

> I didn't react to those words, I didn't take them seriously, they failed to extricate me from my indifference, give me pause, or wrest me from the bench where I sat. I supposed the boy was taunting me and deceiving me for reasons best known to himself, perhaps just to upset me. I was distrustful of everyone and everything, including claims of occurrences that could disturb the daily routine, which was so completely stabilized, in fact ossified. I knew that the arrival of a family member, especially a mother, was one of the incessant dreams the boys lived by, a fantasy irresistible to even the toughest ones, to whom, it might seem, all sentimental daydreams were alien … As for myself, I'd grown deadened … and had most likely lost even the ability to fantasize. Moreover I knew that the world in which I'd … once lived no longer existed, and that behind me was empty space and nothingness. I didn't think about this world, and I didn't return to the past, in an odd way I'd expelled it from my consciousness, and my existence was limited to what was here and now. Nor did I think about whether anyone in my family was alive or whether I would see any of them again.[64]

A few minutes later Sister Róża told Głowiński that his mother was waiting for him in a small room that had once served as a guest room.

There she was. He was "so taken by surprise, so unable to absorb what was happening," that he was speechless. A year and some months before, being separated from her had been a shock. Now their first meeting after a war from which they had "miraculously escaped" with their lives "also came as a shock, in its own way paralyzing." Finally he managed to utter some words: "Mama, a huge louse is marching around your beret."[65] And in fact that was the first thing he noticed.

Paradoxically the louse enabled him to master his overawed state, and "to some extent brought an extraordinary situation into the realm of the ordinary and quotidian." For insects were not foreign to him. He "remembered them from the ghetto, and there was no dearth of them in Turkowice": cockroaches ruled the kitchen, "bedbugs and fleas were everywhere rampant, and … lice enjoyed comfortable lives." His mother, disconcerted no doubt—this was not what she expected after a miserable journey lasting more than two weeks—immediately "took off her old, terribly shabby beret and did away with the insect."[66]

Głowiński could not remember how he parted with his mother—she stayed barely a day—and the boy, suffering "with pus-exuding boils burrowing deeply" into his body, caused by malnutrition, was not able to accompany her. He did know that he was not saying goodbye to her forever. Nor could he remember whether he asked her about his father. He had not seen him for more than two years. He wondered, had he forgotten his existence? For a long time his mother had received no sign of life from her husband, "she knew only that during a roundup in Kielce he had been seized on the street and transported to Germany." That he had survived, the family learned later, "when the war was over and letters could travel back and forth."[67] Near the end of 1945, he made his way back to Poland.

Twice, owing to the state of his health, Głowiński's departure from Turkowice was postponed. After some time his aunt Maria arrived, determined to take him with her. By then, he had recovered somewhat, and they started off. "Packing took not even a minute": he had no things of his own, not even a toothbrush, which during the war had become an unfamiliar object. What he did need was shoes—in summer, he went around barefoot. Sister Róża found the shoes he had been wearing when he arrived. Of course, by now, they were much too small; nonetheless he pushed his "too-big feet" into them. The boy and his aunt arrived back in Pruszków (a rendezvous point for those family members who had managed to survive the occupation) after a difficult journey by way of Chełm and Warsaw. His mother was waiting for him. And at once she set about washing him. "It was an intense scouring," removing the dirt that had accumulated not only during his recent travels but across long years. He asked: "Was it just at this moment that the war and the occupation ended for me?"[68]

* * *

"Without meaning to," Kluger noted, "I find I have written an escape story, not only in the literal sense but in the pejorative sense of the word ... How can I," she continued, "keep my readers from feeling good about the obvious drift of my story away from the gas chambers and the killing fields and towards the postwar period, when prosperity beckons?"[69] Głowiński was not so direct. Yet he shared Kluger's concern lest his audience fail to appreciate the "horror" of the events that he was struggling to bring "back to life."[70]

Kluger proceeded by negative examples. She peppered her memoir with instances of people not listening, not wanting to hear, urging her to forget what had happened: the policeman who, at the war's end, literally put his hands over his ears, the American cousin who told Kluger to erase her past from her memory. And then there were the people who did listen, or made a show of listening, as if she had imposed on them, and they were graciously indulging her. Will her readers tune her out in similar fashion?

Głowiński took a different tack. Where Kluger admonished her audience to listen, he urged his readers to look. He created scenes so clearly realized, he described them in such graphic detail, that readers could summon them up in their mind's eye. Will they avert their gaze?

"Hier ist kein warum" (There Is No Why Here): Primo Levi

In Monowitz-Buna—the satellite camp of Auschwitz to which he was deported in February 1944—Primo Levi had a recurrent nightmare. A group is gathered; his younger sister is there. "They are all listening," so it seems. He speaks about "our hunger and about how we are checked for lice, and about the Kapo who hit" him. "It is an intense pleasure, … inexpressible, to be at home, among friendly people, and to have so many things to recount." But he cannot help noticing that his audience does not follow him. "In fact, they are completely indifferent": they chat among themselves as if he were not there. His sister looks at him, "gets up, and goes away without a word." Levi asks himself: "Why does it happen? Why is the pain of every day so constantly translated … into the repeated scene of the story told and not listened to?"[1]

Once back in Turin, after a nine-month odyssey, north, east, west, and finally south, Levi likened himself to Samuel Taylor Coleridge's Ancient Mariner. He shared a narrative impulse, indeed a compulsion: the Ancient Mariner tells his tale to the wedding guests as they arrive, and they snub him; Levi relates his story to whomever he meets, including strangers on trains. Then he put pen to paper and composed his first book. To the end of his life, Levi was loath to acknowledge that he had produced a work of literature.[2]

Its merits were not immediately appreciated. Natalia Ginzburg—a distinguished writer in the making—rejected it for publication by Einaudi of Turin. She judged it not right for Einaudi's list. Or was the time not right in 1947? A number of other publishers turned it down as well. Levi revised, polished, and at last found a home for the work entitled *Se questo è un uomo* (*If This Is a Man*). Over the next decade, little by little, Levi's slim volume established itself; in 1958 Einaudi reversed its earlier decision and from then on published all of his writings. In 1961 a paperback English translation appeared—with the misleading title *Survival in Auschwitz*.

On his return to Turin, Levi had settled into the apartment, on Corso Re Umberto, where, in 1919, he had been born; where, in the postwar years, he raised his own family; and where, in 1987, he committed suicide. His family was solidly bourgeois—and secular. Like many of his generation of Italian Jews, he had paid no particular attention to his Jewishness before 1938, that is, before Mussolini's anti-Semitic legislation. Until then he had regarded his origin as a "nearly negligible but curious fact, a small, cheerful anomaly, like ... having freckles." Until then he had thought of a Jew as "someone who doesn't have a Christmas tree, who shouldn't eat salami but eats it anyway, who learned a little Hebrew at the age of thirteen and then forgot it." His Christian classmates were, and continued to be, civil people, and "neither they nor the professors ... directed a hostile word or gesture" at him. Still, he could feel them withdraw, and he withdrew as well: "each look exchanged ... was accompanied by a tiny but perceptible flash of distrust and suspicion."[3]

Now Levi faced the problem of continuing his studies. At an early age he had determined to become a chemist. By November 1938, when the bulk of the anti-Semitic laws went into effect, he was a second-year university student— and a proviso allowed Jews at this stage of their training to finish their courses. An assistantship, crucial to the successful completion of his degree, was another matter. After being repeatedly rebuffed, Levi found a junior faculty member willing to take him on. And so, during the early months of 1941, as "the Germans destroyed Belgrade, broke the Greek resistance, invaded Crete from the air," Levi stuck to his task of purifying benzene and preparing for an unknown, yet ominous, future.[4] That June, just as the Germans launched their invasion of the Soviet Union, he received his doctor's degree, *summa cum laude*.

For the next two years, Levi lived by odd jobs, working illegally under a false non-Jewish surname. In Milan, where employment took him, he encountered militant anti-Fascism and began his own anti-Fascist education. During the winter 1942–3, with the Allied landings in North Africa, the Soviet resistance, and finally victory at Stalingrad, "men whom fascism had not bowed, lawyers, professors, and workers ... came out of the shadows." They explained to Levi and his friends that "fascism was not only a clownish and improvident … government," that "it not only had dragged Italy into an ill-omened and unjust war," but that it was "based on coercion of those who work, on uncontrolled profits for those who exploit the work of others, on silence imposed on those who think and don't wish to be slaves, on systematic and calculated lies." Their education was interrupted. Events supervened: in March came the strikes in Turin; on July 25 came the collapse of Fascism, thanks to a palace intrigue; "and then came September 8, the gray-green serpent of Nazi divisions in the streets of Milan and Turin, the brutal awakening … Italy was an occupied country, like Poland, like Yugoslavia, like Norway."[5]

Levi fled to the hills of his native Piedmont—with the aim of setting up a partisan unit affiliated with the non-communist resistance movement Justice and Liberty. No easy task: the band lacked "capable men," and was swamped instead by "a deluge of outcasts who, in good and bad faith, came … in search on a nonexistent organization, commanders, weapons, or merely protection, a fire, a pair of shoes."[6] On December 13, 1943, Levi and his comrades found themselves surrounded by Fascist militia. They had been betrayed. Levi managed to hide the tiny revolver he kept under his pillow—in any case he was not sure how to use it. His interrogator hammered away for hours without rest. "He wanted to know everything. He continuously threatened torture" and the firing squad, "but luckily I knew almost nothing, and the names I did know I kept to myself. He alternated moments of simulated cordiality with equally simulated bursts of anger … He said (probably bluffing) that he knew I was Jewish, but that was good for me: either I was a Jew or I was a partisan; if a partisan, he would shoot me; if a Jew, fine, there was a collection camp …, I would remain there until the ultimate victory."[7] Levi admitted to being a Jew.

By February 1944, he was on the train to Auschwitz. The eleven months of his captivity provided him the impetus and the material for his writing career—a career that for decades he pursued alongside that of industrial chemist. "Primo Levi the writer," he claimed, owed "a debt … to Primo Levi the chemist." For him, "chemistry wasn't only a profession, it was … the source of certain mental habits, above all that of clarity."[8] He saw in the Lager (concentration camp; German: Konzentrationslager—KL) "a gigantic biological and social experiment," and he reported on it with precision and without sentimentality.[9] He focused on his experience not because it was his, rather because it helped to explain an anomaly—his very survival.

Lucid and economical, yes. But also subtlety ironic. Note the first sentence of *If This Is a Man*: "It was my good fortune to be deported to Auschwitz only in 1944."[10] (Literally true: by then the shortage of manpower in Germany had led the Nazis to extend the life of concentration camp prisoners.) The unexpectedness of this opening—what fortune is it to have been deported to Auschwitz—underlines the sense of sheer arbitrariness. Levi was no more deserving of what happened to him—for good and for ill—than anyone else. "After my return from the camps," he wrote, "I received a visit from an older friend, ... a follower of his own personal religion ... He was happy to find me alive and, for the most part, unharmed ... He told me that my survival could not be the result of chance, ... but was ... the work of Providence. I was one of the elect, the chosen: I, the nonbeliever, and even less of a believer after my time in Auschwitz, had been saved, touched by Grace."[11] Such an opinion seemed monstrous to Levi. If there was a reason for choosing him, it was an inadequate one. "'*Hier ist kein warum*' (there is no why here)," so barked an Auschwitz guard as he snatched away an icicle from a desperately thirsty Levi.[12] And Levi offers no demurral: he offers no neat or tidy explanation. With the ironic tone of the opening sentence, he begins a mediation on luck and fortune—in all their specificity.

"The demolition of a man"

Winter, intense cold. "*Wieviel Stück?*" the SS officer demanded. "The corporal saluted smartly and replied that there were six hundred and fifty 'pieces,' and all was in order."[13] The people, 650 men, women, and children, were then loaded onto freight cars. The oldest was over eighty, the youngest three months old. Many were ill, and some seriously; an old man who had recently suffered a cerebral hemorrhage was, nonetheless, dragged onto the train. He died en route. During that four-day journey, a single daily halt gave the prisoners a chance to get down from the train and pick up handfuls of snow. They were given some food, bread, jam, cheese, but never water or anything else to drink.[14] Destination: Auschwitz, a name still without significance for Levi.

"The climax came suddenly. The door opened with a crash ... A vast platform appeared ..., illuminated by floodlights ... A dozen SS men stood to one side, legs apart, with a look of indifference." They began to move among the new arrivals and "in low voices, with faces of stone," started to interrogate them rapidly, "in bad Italian ... 'How old? Healthy or ill?' And on the basis of the reply they pointed ... in two different directions." Ninety-six men and twenty-nine women were selected for work. (Of those ninety-six, only fifteen survived, and of the twenty-nine women, eight returned home.[15]) The remaining 526 were murdered forthwith—without ever being registered as camp inmates. "In an instant, our women, our parents, our children disappeared. We saw them for a short while as a dark mass at the ... end of the platform; then we saw nothing more."[16]

Levi and the other men were dispatched to Monowitz-Buna. Typically Jewish prisoners toiled away for SS enterprises, private companies, or the Nazi state. In this case they were drudges in the service of IG Farben. Early in the spring of 1941, Auschwitz prisoners had been sent to start building a factory to produce a kind of rubber called Buna. At first the prisoners slept in the main camp; so they had to march every day for several hours along muddy roads, to and from the building site, roughly four miles away. IG Farben managers blamed these exhausting treks for the prisoners' poor output and lobblied for a satellite camp right next to the factory. In the summer of 1942, construction of the Monowitz (or Buna) camp began, and it opened three months later. In all there were eight compounds on the enormous IG Farben site. Some workers, "like German civilians, enjoyed comparatively good conditions"; others, like forced laborers from the Soviet Union, suffered terribly. "The KL, ... the only compound run by the SS, was the worst." And it quickly grew in size: at the beginning of 1943, there were already 3,750 prisoners, increasing to approximately 7,000 a year later. "The great majority of them—around nine out of ten—were Jews." Yet "despite the investment of hundreds of millions of Reichsmark and the abuse of tens of thousands of slave laborers, the huge IG Farben complex ... was never completed and failed to produce any synthetic rubber."[17]

The journey, by truck, from Auschwitz to Monowitz lasted no more than twenty minutes. Levi soon found himself in a huge, empty room. An SS man enters. He inquires, "*Wer kann Deutsch?*" Someone steps forward to translate. "We are to form rows of five ...; then we are to undress and make a bundle of our clothes in a particular way, the woolen garments on one side, all the rest on the other; we must take off our shoes but pay careful attention not to let them be stolen." Stolen, by whom, Levi wonders. "And what about our documents, the few things we have in our pockets ...? We all look at the interpreter, and the interpreter asks the German, and the German smokes and looks right through him, as if he were transparent, as if no one had spoken." Imagine, Levi addresses his reader, "a man who has been deprived of everyone he loves, and at the same time of his house, his habits, his clothes, ... in short, of literally everything ... that he possesses: he will be a hollow man, reduced to suffering and needs, heedless of dignity and restraint, for he who loses everything can easily lose himself ... Language lacks words to express this offense, the demolition of a man."[18]

Then, the "real, true initiation": Levi is tattooed. He becomes Häftling 174517. The numbers themselves recount "the stages of destruction of European Judaism." To the old hands of the camp, they told everything: "The period of entry into the camp, the convoy one belonged to, and, consequently, the nationality. Everyone will treat with respect the numbers 30000 to 80000: there are only a few hundred left and they represent the survivors of the Polish ghettos ... As for the high numbers, there is something essentially comic about them ... The typical high number is a corpulent, docile, and stupid fellow: you can make him believe that at the infirmary leather shoes are distributed to all those with delicate feet, and ... you can send him to the most ferocious of the Kapos to ask him (as happened to me!) if it is true that his is the *Kartoffelschalenkommando*, the Potato Peeling Unit, and if it's possible to enroll in it."[19]

Rites and rituals needed to be learned quickly. They were many and complicated—and senseless. For example: "Every morning you have to make the 'bed' perfectly flat and smooth; smear your muddy and repellent clogs with the appropriate machine grease; scrape the mud stains off your clothes (paint, grease, and rust stains, however, are permitted). In the evening you have to be checked for lice ...; on Saturday, you have your beard and hair shaved, mend your rags or have them mended; on Sunday, there is a general check for skin diseases and a check for the number of buttons on your jacket, which should be five." There were countless prohibitions as well: "To sleep in one's jacket, or without one's pants, or with one's cap on; to use certain washrooms or latrines, which are *nur für Kapos* or *nur für Reichsdeutsche*; not to have a shower on the prescribed day, or to have one on a day not prescribed; to leave the barrack with one's jacket unbuttoned, or with the collar raised; to wear paper or straw under one's clothes against the cold; to wash except stripped to the waist."[20]

Then there were a host of things that under normal circumstances could have been handled easily, but not so in the Lager. For instance: "if you go to the latrine or washroom, everything has to be carried along, always and everywhere, and while you wash your face the bundle of clothes has to be held tightly between your knees," otherwise it will be stolen in a second; "if a shoe hurts, you have to show up in the evening at the ceremony of the shoe exchange"—this tests the skill of the individual who, "in the midst of an incredible throng, has to be able to choose at a glance one (not a pair, one) shoe that fits. Because, once the choice is made," there can be no second exchange. And the matter of shoes should not be dismissed lightly. "Death," Levi wrote, "begins with the shoes: for most of us, they prove to be instruments of torture, which after a few hours of marching cause painful sores that become fatally infected. Anyone who has them is forced to walk as if he were dragging a ball and chain …; he arrives last everywhere, and everywhere he receives blows … His feet swell, and the more they swell, the more unbearable the friction with the wood and cloth of the shoes becomes. Then only the hospital is left: but to enter the hospital with a diagnosis of *dicke Füsse* (swollen feet) is extremely dangerous, because it is well known to all, and especially to the SS, that there is no cure here for that complaint."[21]

As for work—"in its turn, a tangle of laws, taboos, and problems." All hours of daylight were work hours: 8 to 12 and 12:30 to 4 in winter; 6:30 to 12 and 1 to 6 in summer. Every other Sunday was a regular workday; "on the so-called holiday Sundays, instead of working at Buna," the prisoners usually worked "on the upkeep of the Lager, so that days of actual rest" were extremely rare. Divided into about 200 Kommandos, with between 15 and 150 men each and supervised by a Kapo, the prisoners set out in the morning for Buna and returned to the camp in the evening. There were "good and bad Kommandos," which, for the most part, were used as transport, and the work was hard, very hard in the winter. There were "also skilled Kommandos (electricians, smiths, bricklayers, welders, mechanics, concrete layers, etc.), each attached to a specific workshop or section of Buna, and answering more directly to civilian foremen … The assignment of individuals to the various Kommandos" was "organized by a special office of the Lager, the *Arbeitsdienst*," which was in "constant touch with the civilian management of Buna."[22] Favoritism ran rampant.

Nights offered little rest. Levi's companion—the prisoners slept two to a bunk, and the bunk itself was little more than two feet wide—"wraps himself in the blanket" they share, shoves Levi "aside with a blow from his bony hips, turns his back … and begins to snore." Levi struggles "to regain a reasonable area of the straw mattress": first, back-to-back, he pushes against his bedmate's lower back; then he turns around and uses his knees; finally he takes hold of the other man's ankles and tries to move them farther from his face. "Lying like this, forced into immobility, half on the bunk's edge," Levi falls into a sleep so light that he cannot screen out "the movement to and from the bucket next to the night guard." (Every two or three hours the prisoners have to get up to eliminate the large quantities of liquid they consume daily in the form of soup.) "The old inhabitants of the camp have refined their senses to such a degree that, while still in their bunks, they are miraculously able to distinguish if the level is at a dangerous point, purely on the basis of the sound that the sides of the bucket make—with the result that they almost always manage to avoid emptying it." So the candidates for bucket service are the inexperienced new arrivals. "When need drives us to the bucket …, the night guard grabs us, scribbles down our number, hands us a pair of wooden clogs and the bucket, and chases us out into the snow, shivering and sleepy. It is our task to trudge to the latrine with the bucket, which knocks against our … calves; … inevitably with the shaking, some of the contents spills over our feet."[23]

Within a fortnight, Levi finds himself "on the bottom."

> Already my body is no longer mine; my belly is swollen, my limbs emaciated, my face is puffy in the morning and hollow in the evening; some of us have yellow skin, others gray. When we don't meet for three or four days we scarcely recognize one another.
>
> We Italians had decided to gather every Sunday in a corner of the Lager, but we stopped at once, because it was too sad to count our numbers and find, each time, that we were fewer and more disfigured and desolate. And it was so tiring to walk those few steps: and then, upon meeting, we would remember and think, and it was better not to.[24]

* * *

How, then, did Levi survive? As he saw it, there were "two particularly well differentiated categories"—the drowned and the saved. To sink was the easiest thing: one had "to carry out all ... orders ..., eat only the rations, stick to the discipline of the work and the camp. Experience proved that very rarely could one survive more than three months in this way. All the Muselmänner"—the term used by the old timers to describe the weak, the inept, those doomed to selection—"have the same story, or more exactly, have no story ... Once they entered the camp, they were overwhelmed, either through basic incapacity, or through misfortune, or through some banal incident," before they could adapt: "They do not begin to learn German"—Levi appreciated full well that the rudimentary German he had picked up as a student was a lifesaver; they do not begin "to untangle the fiendish knot of laws and prohibitions until their body is already breaking down ... Their life is short, but their number is endless; they, ... the drowned, form the backbone of the camp, an anonymous mass, ... of non-men who march and labor in silence, ... already too empty to suffer. One hesitates to call them living; one hesitates to call their death death—in the face of it they have no fear, because they are too tired to understand."[25]

Null Achtzehn—Zero Eighteen, the only Muselmann Levi summons up specifically—is known by the last three digits of his entry number, "as if everyone were aware that only a man is worthy of a name, and that Null Achtzehn is no longer a man." For all that, he is young, very young, which itself is a grave danger. "Not only because it's harder for boys than for men to withstand fatigue and fasting but, even more, because long training in the struggle of each against all is needed to survive" in Auschwitz, "training that young people rarely have." Null Achtzehn is not even particularly weak, "but he doesn't have the sense" to avoid excess effort. So he is the one who works more than anybody else, and he is the one nobody wants to work with. When thinking of him, Levi is reminded "of the sled dogs in books by Jack London, who labor until their last breath and die on the track."[26]

If the drowned have no story, "and there is only a single broad path to perdition, the paths to salvation are many, rugged and unimaginable."[27]

Some general remarks. Prominenz figured as the principal way to survival. Prominenten was "the name for camp officials, from the ... [senior camp inmate] (*Lagerältester*) to the Kapos, the cooks, the nurses, the night guards, even the barrack sweepers, and the *Scheissminister* and *Bademeister* (superintendents of the latrines and the showers)." Jewish Prominenten was among the most asocial and insensitive. They understood that if they were not sufficiently cruel and tyrannical, someone else, someone judged more suitable, would take over their posts. Besides these officials, there was the vast number of prisoners who had to "battle every day and every hour against exhaustion, hunger, and the resulting inertia," who had to resist enemies and show no pity for rivals, who had "to strangle all dignity and kill all conscience, to enter the arena as a beast against other beasts ... To survive without renouncing any part of their own moral world ... was conceded only to a very few superior individuals, made of the stuff of martyrs and saints."[28]

A striking example: Alfred L.—his real name was Alfred Fisch.[29] Before the war he had been "the manager of an extremely important factory that made chemical products, and his name was ... familiar in industrial circles throughout Europe." But he had entered the camp—at roughly age fifty—"like everyone else: naked, alone, and unknown." When Levi encountered him, "he was very emaciated, yet his face still preserved the features of a ... methodical energy; at the time, his privileges were limited to the daily cleaning of the Polish workers' soup vat; this job, which he had somehow obtained as his exclusive monopoly, yielded him half a bowlful of soup per day. Certainly it was not enough to satisfy his hunger; nevertheless, no one had ever heard him complain."[30]

L.'s plan for survival was "a long-term one, which is all the more remarkable as it was conceived in an environment dominated by a mentality of the provisional; and L. carried it out with strict inner discipline, and without pity for himself or—with greater reason—for comrades who crossed his path. L. knew ... that everywhere, and especially amid the general leveling of the Lager, a respectable appearance is the best guarantee of being respected." He kept his hands and face perfectly clean, "he had the rare self-denial to wash his shirt every fortnight, without waiting for the bimonthly change (... to wash a shirt meant finding soap, finding time, finding space in an overcrowded washhouse; training oneself to keep careful watch on the wet shirt, without losing sight of it for a moment, and to put it on, naturally still wet, at the time for silence, when the lights are turned out)"; even his striped garments were unsoiled and new. "L. had acquired ... the ... [look] of a Prominent, considerably before becoming one." Only much later did Levi learn "that he had been able to earn all this show of prosperity with incredible tenacity, paying for each of his acquisitions … with bread from his own ration, thus imposing on himself a regime of additional privations."[31]

L.'s chance came when the Chemical Kommando was formed. (More about that shortly.) "He needed no more than his tidy clothing and his … clean-shaved face amid the herd of his sordid and slovenly colleagues to convince both Kapo and *Arbeitsdienst* immediately that he was one of the genuinely saved, a potential Prominent, and so … he was, of course, promoted to 'specialist,' named technical head of the Kommando, and taken on by the management of Buna as an analyst in the laboratory of the Styrene Department. He was subsequently appointed to examine all the new additions to the Chemical Kommando staff, in order to judge their professional ability. He … did this with extreme rigor," always on the alert for a possible rival."[32]

Levi never learned how his story continued. He assumed that L. had escaped death and that he was still living his cold and joyless existence.

* * *

"If I am alive today," Levi maintained, "I owe it to Lorenzo."[33] A master bricklayer by trade, Lorenzo was a forced laborer. In 1939 he had been employed by an Italian company that did business in France. When war broke out, he had been interned, and when the Germans arrived, he along with all his co-workers had been shipped off to Upper Silesia. There they lived like soldiers, housed in barracks, with Sundays off and a week or two of holidays, paid in marks, allowed to communicate with Italy, to send remittances and to receive packages of clothes and food. He and Levi "belonged to different orders of the Nazi universe."[34]

Levi met Lorenzo in June 1944. A bombing raid had smashed up a site where both of them worked; it had damaged buildings and also delicate machinery that would be needed when—or if—the Buna factory entered the production phase. The most valuable items were, in future, to be protected by thick brick walls. Lorenzo's team was assigned the job of constructing them, and Levi's squad had the task of fetching and carrying. As luck would have it, Levi was sent to be Lorenzo's helper.

It was a crime for a prisoner and a civilian to talk to one another: the prisoner risked a trial for spying; the civilian risked ending up a camp inmate, albeit for a fixed term. Levi warned Lorenzo of the danger he was running; Lorenzo just "shrugged his shoulders and said nothing"—he was a man of few words. "He didn't speak, but he understood," Levi wrote. "Two or three days after our encounter, he brought me an Alpine division mess pail . . . full of soup, and told me to bring it back empty before evening. From then on the soup was always there, sometimes along with a piece of bread. He brought it to me every day for six months."[35]

An even more serious crime: Lorenzo mailed a postcard on Levi's behalf. Levi had found an opportunity to draft a message—"clear enough" for his family and "yet so innocent that it wouldn't rouse the attention of the censors."[36] Lorenzo copied it; signed it in his own name and sent it to Italy. Two months later, Lorenzo brought Levi "an extraordinary gift"—a letter from home, an "unheard-of-event." For all this, Lorenzo "neither asked nor accepted any reward." He did not think "that one should do good for a reward."[37]

And thanks to Lorenzo's humanity, Levi "managed not to forget" that he himself "was a man."[38]

* * *

Like L., Levi was taken into the Chemical Kommando. Kommando 98, as the work squad was known, had nothing to do with chemistry in the laboratory sense: it was a heavy-transport detail attached to a magnesium chloride warehouse. In early July Levi heard a rumor: "specialists" were needed in the camp's synthetic rubber plants. Now Levi saw his chance. But to become a specialist he has to pass an examination—in German—set by Dr. Wilhelm Pannwitz of the polymerization department.

Levi is ushered into the room:

> Pannwitz is tall, thin, blond; he has the eyes, the hair, and the nose that all Germans ought to have, and sits formidably behind an elaborate desk. I, Häftling 174517, stand in his office, shining, clean, orderly, and it seems to me that I would leave a dirty stain if I were to touch anything.
>
> When he finished writing, he raised his eyes and looked at me. . . .
>
> What we all thought and said of the Germans could be felt at that moment, in an immediate manner. The brain that governed those blue eyes and those manicured hands said, "This something in front of me belongs to a species that it is obviously right to suppress. In this particular case, one has first to make sure it does not contain some useful element."

The examination begins:

> "*Wo sind Sie geboren?*" He uses *Sie*, the polite form of address.... .
>
> "I took my degree at Turin in 1941, *summa cum laude*"—and, as I say
> it, I have the definite impression of not being believed. I don't really believe
> it myself; it is enough to look at my dirty hands covered with sores, my
> convict's trousers encrusted with mud. Yet I am ... the university graduate of
> Turin—in fact ... even after this long period of idleness ... my reservoir of
> knowledge of organic chemistry ... responds upon request with unexpected
> docility. And, even more, this sense of lucid elation, this excitement which
> I feel warm my veins, I recognize it, it is the fever of exams, *my* fever of
> *my* exams, the spontaneous mobilization of all my logical faculties and my
> knowledge that my classmates so envied.[39]

The examination is over; it has gone well. Yet nothing changes.

Summer turns into autumn. Levi and the other "chemists" drag around
phenyl beta sacks. With the start of the air raids, they clear out the warehouse;
when there is a pause in the air attack, they move the sacks back into the
warehouse; then when the warehouse is actually hit, they lug the sacks into the
cellar of the styrene department; and, finally, after the warehouse is repaired,
they pile the sacks in there once more. All the while the phenyl beta is getting
under their clothes, sticking to their sweaty limbs, and eating away at their skin.
"So far," Levi noted, "the advantages of being in the Chemical Kommando have
been limited to the following: the others have received coats and we have not;
the others carry fifty-kilo sacks of cement, while we carry sixty-kilo sacks of
phenyl beta. How can we still think about the chemistry examination and the
illusions of that time?"[40]

* * *

With the approach of winter, Levi sensed selections in the air. Months earlier
the Germans had constructed two large tents in an open space in the Lager.
Throughout the spring and summer, each of them housed more than a
thousand men; now the tents have been taken down, and those men have been
crammed into the existing barracks. Levi and other old timers know that the
Germans do not like such disorder and that soon something would be done to
reduce the numbers.

"The atmosphere of the Lager and the worksite," Levi wrote, "is saturated
with *Selekcja*"—a hybrid Latin and Polish word. "In the latrines, in the

washhouse, we show each other our chests, our buttocks, our thighs, and our comrades reassure us: 'You'll be all right, it certainly won't be your turn this time … *du bist kein Muselmann.*'"

> I brazenly lied to old Wertheimer; I told him that if they questioned him, he should say he's forty-five … It's absurd for Wertheimer to hope; he looks sixty, he has enormous varicose veins, he hardly notices hunger anymore. But he lies down on his bed, serene and quiet, and replies to anyone who asks with my words; they are the watchword in the camp these days … Except for the details—I heard them said to me by Chaim, who has been in the Lager for three years, and … is wonderfully sure of himself; and I believed him.[41]

The day is a working Sunday. At 1:00 p.m., the prisoners return to camp "for a shower, shaving, and the general inspection for skin diseases and lice." Then the bell sounds signaling confinement to barracks. The Blockältester, the senior block inmate, after making sure that everyone is inside, hands each prisoner the card that bears his name, number, profession, age, and nationality and orders him to undress completely, except for shoes. Under a barrage of shouts, oaths, and blows, the prisoners are herded into the Tagesraum—a small room, seven-by-four meters—which is the quartermaster's office. The door between the Tagesraum and the dormitory is locked; the doors to the outside from both the Tagesraum and the dormitory are open. Between these two open doors stand the SS officer in charge, the Blockältester, and the quartermaster.

> Each of us, as he comes naked out of the Tagesraum into the cold … air, has to run … in front of the three men, give the card to the SS officer, and go back through the dormitory door. The SS officer, in … [a] fraction of a second …, with a glance at front and back, judges our fate, and in turn gives the card to the man on the right or his left, and this is life or death of each of us … Like everyone else, I passed by with a brisk and elastic step, trying to keep my head high, my chest forward, and my muscles taut and conspicuous. Out of the corner of my eye I tried to look back, and it seemed to me that my card ended up on the right.[42]

In three or four minutes, the barrack is done.

Naturally, there have been some irregularities: "René, for example, so young, ended up on the left; perhaps it's because he has glasses, perhaps because he walks with a slight stoop, like someone who is nearsighted, but more likely it was a simple error." It must also have been a mistake with "Sattler, a huge Transylvanian peasant who was still at home only twenty days ago; Sattler does not know German, has understood nothing of what has happened."[43]

And so, in this arbitrary fashion, the drowned and the saved have, once again, been sorted out.

That evening, from his bunk on the top level, Levi hears and sees "old Kuhn praying aloud, with his cap on his head, his torso swaying violently. Kuhn is thanking God that he was not chosen."

> Kuhn is out of his mind. Does he not see, in the bunk next to him, Beppo the Greek, who is twenty years old and is going to the gas chamber the day after tomorrow, and knows it, and lies there staring at the light without saying anything ...? Does Kuhn not know that next time it will be his turn? Does Kuhn not understand that what happened today is an abomination, which no propitiatory prayer, no pardon, no expiation by the guilty—nothing at all in the power of man to do—can ever heal?
>
> If I were God, I would spit Kuhn's prayer out upon the ground.[44]

* * *

Winter is coming—and so too are the Russians. "Every day the ... [air-raid sirens} wail ... The electric power plant isn't running, the methanol rectification columns no longer exist, three of the four acetylene gasometers have been blown up." One morning the Kapo announces: "Doktor Pannwitz has communicated to the *Arbeitsdienst* that three Häftlinge have been chosen for the Laboratory." Levi, one of those chosen, is handed a ticket: it says "Häftling 174517, as a specialized worker, has the right to a new shirt and underpants and must be shaved every Wednesday." With the ravaged Buna "lying under the first snow, silent and stiff, like an enormous corpse," Levi has been promoted.[45]

He has taken a huge step up the ladder of privilege. In the camp, at night and in the morning, nothing distinguishes the three specialists from the rest of the Chemical Kommando. But during the day they work in a laboratory—surprisingly like any other laboratory, with "three long workbenches covered with hundreds of familiar objects." Can what he does even be called work? "To work," Levi insisted, "is to push carts, carry [railroad] ties, break stones, shovel earth, grip with bare hands the repugnant iciness of frozen iron."[46] Whereas he sits all day; he has paper and pencil, and he has been given a book to refresh his memory of chemical analysis.

Levi is doubly privileged: he has escaped the harsh winter weather; and he assumes that the problem of hunger will not be too difficult to solve. He asks rhetorically: "Will they really want to search us every day when we leave? And, even if they do, what about every time we ask to go to the latrine? Obviously not. And there is soap, gas, alcohol here." He plans "to stitch a secret pocket inside ... [his] jacket, and make a deal with the Englishman [a POW] who works in the repair shop and trades in gas ... I have spent a year in the Lager and I know that if one wants to steal and seriously sets one's mind to it, no searches and no supervision can prevent it."[47]

Privileged yes, but also "repulsive." That is how Levi imagined he was being judged by the young German girls in the laboratory.

> We know what we look like: we see one another and sometimes we happen to see our own reflection in a ... window ... Our heads are bald on Monday, and covered by a short light-brown mold by Saturday. We have swollen, yellow faces, permanently marked by the cuts of the hasty barber, and often by bruises and numb sores; our necks are long and knobbly, like plucked chickens. Our clothes are incredibly filthy, stained with mud, grease, and blood ... Our wooden clogs are intolerably noisy and are encrusted with alternate layers of mud and regulation grease ... We are full of fleas, and often scratch ourselves shamelessly; we have to go to the latrine with humiliating frequency.[48]

His privileged position Levi considered "a gift of fate"—but there was no guarantee about tomorrow. He could be certain of one thing: "At the first piece of glassware I break, the first measurement error, the first failure to pay attention, I will go back to waste away in the snow and wind until I, too, am ready for the chimney."[49]

January 1945

Working in the chemical laboratory, Levi stole small, unusual objects—and "therefore of high trade value"—which he hoped to swap for food. Pipettes— "slender, graduated glass tubes used to transfer precise quantities of liquid from one receptacle to another"—suited his purposes. Levi offered his booty to a Polish nurse assigned to the infectious diseases ward. As payment, a disappointed Levi received only a half-full bowl of soup. "Who would have left half a bowl of soup ...? Almost certainly someone who was gravely ill, and, given the setting, also contagious." That same evening Levi shared his soup with his friend Alberto—a friend whom Levi described as his "alter ego."[50]

Alberto and Levi were roughly the same age and height; they even looked somewhat alike. Their "foreign companions ... considered it superfluous to distinguish" between them, and "expected that when they called 'Alberto!' or 'Primo!' whoever was closest would answer."[51] When Levi was chosen to work in the chemical laboratory, Alberto was the first to congratulate him—both because of their friendship and because he would gain from it. The two of them were "bound by a very close alliance, under which every 'organized' scrap of food" was divided equally.[52] And so they shared the suspect soup.

A few days later, Levi woke with a high fever, scarcely able to swallow. He was admitted to the infirmary. This turned out to be a huge stroke of luck. Alberto, who had had scarlet fever as a child, was among the more than 50,000 prisoners herded westward.[53]

An estimated 15,000 men, women, and children from the abandoned Auschwitz complex perished during the evacuation of early 1945. Privileged prisoners fared better: they wore proper shoes and warm clothes. Others staggered along in rags and wooden clogs, and soon collapsed. Illness and exhaustion may have been the main killers, but shootings took their toll. Anyone suspected of trying to escape was fair game—even prisoners who had merely stepped out to defecate by the side of the road. The victims died a lonely death, felled by SS bullets after they had lost touch with the main column. The perpetrators were usually not senior camp SS officers—most of the local top brass had already made their getaway. The supervision of the march was in the hands of underlings, leaving it up to each guard whether to pull the trigger.[54]

"On the night of January 18," Levi wrote, "Alberto came, defying the prohibition, to say good-bye ... from the window ... It didn't take many words ... We did not think that we would be separated for very long. He had found a pair of sturdy leather shoes in fairly good condition ... He ... was cheerful and confident ... It was understandable: ... we could concretely feel that hated world of ours on the verge of collapse."[55] Like thousands of others, Alberto died on the march.

* * *

Levi remained too sick to tramp through the snow. He estimated that there were approximately 800 left behind to await the Russians. "With the rhythm of the great machine of the Lager extinguished, for us began the days outside the world and time."[56] This final phase of survival, unguarded and forsaken in the bitter January cold, was the only one Levi narrated in full grisly detail. "For a reason both moral and aesthetic: this was when the Nazis … broke the spirit even of those who had held out until then."[57] And without Charles and Arthur, Levi, too, would have succumbed.

These two French non-Jews had been in the Lager less than a month and "hardly suffered from hunger."[58] The three on them joined forces and formed a salvage team.

Four items stand out. First came heat. When the camp was abandoned, so too was the central heating plant. Outside it must have been −20°C; inside the temperature was dropping hour by hour. Levi "felt ill and helpless … But Charles was courageous and robust, while Arthur was shrewd and had a peasant's practical common sense." Together they set out "into the wind of a freezing, foggy day, clumsily wrapped in blankets." In the ruins of the kitchens they spied what they were looking for: "a heavy cast-iron stove, with a flue still usable."[59] On the way back to the room, they found wood and coal and embers from burned barracks. Despite their hands being numb with cold and the icy metal sticking to their fingers, they managed to get the stove to work. And it began to spread heat.

Second: light. Levi "went to the former clinic, searching for anything that might be useful." Others had been there already: "everything had been smashed by inexpert looters. Not a bottle was intact, on the floor a layer of rags, excrement, and bandages, a naked, contorted corpse." Yet here was something that had escaped notice: a truck battery. Levi "touched the poles with a knife—a small spark. It was charged."[60] That evening his room had light.

Third: food. There had been a distribution of bread before the SS departed, and, in ransacking the kitchens in search of a stove, Levi and his friends had managed to fill two sacks with potatoes. As for water, they melted snow, "a tortuous operation in the absence of large containers, and yielding a blackish, muddy liquid that had to be filtered." Then they discovered piles of cabbages and turnips. The next order of business was to make soup. There was enough for the prisoners in Levi's room, who "greedily devoured" it, but not for "the crowd of the semi-living," who, having heard that soup was cooking, "gathered at the door."[61]

Fourth: sanitation. The other inhabitants of Levi's room—there were eleven altogether, one died before the Russians arrived, five others shortly after liberation—were suffering from scarlet fever, typhus, diphtheria, all highly contagious. It hadn't occurred to Levi that he might "go to another room, in another barrack, with less danger of infection." Here, he reflected, was warmth; here was light; here he had a bed; and "ties that bound ... the ... patients of the *Infektionsabteilung.*" By the time they had wolfed down their first soup, Levi had begun to appreciate how awful it would be to let themselves "be submerged now." He told the sick men first in French, then in his "best German, that they should ... think about returning home, and that ... certain things had to be done and others avoided. Each of ... [them] should carefully look after his own bowl and spoon; no one should offer to others any soup that he might have left over; no one should get out of bed except to go to the latrine; anyone who was in need of anything should turn" to the three of them." Levi "had the impression" that they "were too indifferent to everything to pay attention."[62]

Levi punctuated his narrative of resourceful improvisation with visions of the "drowning"—and his own despair.

> Only a wooden wall separated us from the ward of the dysentery patients, where many were dying and many were dead ... None of the sick men had strength enough to come out from under their blankets to search for food, and those who had done so earlier had not returned to help their comrades. In one bed next to the partition, clinging to each other to better withstand the cold, there were two Italians. I often heard them talking, but, since I was speaking only French, for a long time they were not aware of my presence ... [Then] by chance they heard my name, pronounced by Charles with an Italian accent, and from then on they never ceased groaning and pleading.
>
> Naturally I would have liked to help them, given the means and the strength, if for no other reason than to stop their obsessive howls. In the evening, when all the work was done, I overcame fatigue and disgust, and dragged myself to their ward, groping my way along the dark, filthy corridor,

with a bowl of water and the remainder of the day's soup. The result was that from then on, through the thin wall, the whole diarrhea ward called my name, day and night, in the accents of all the languages of Europe, accompanied by incomprehensible prayers, I could bring them no relief. I felt close to tears, I could have cursed them.

Under the date January 26, Levi penned his most anguished lines:

> We were lying in a world of dead men and phantoms. The last trace of civilization had vanished around and inside us. The work of bestial degradation, begun by the Germans in triumph had been brought to its conclusion by the Germans in defeat.
>
> It is man who kills, who creates or suffers injustice; he who shares his bed with a corpse, having lost all restraint, is not a man. He who has waited for his neighbor to die in order to take his piece of bread is, albeit blameless, farther from the model of thinking man than ... the most vicious sadist.[63]

On January 27, Levi spotted the first Russian patrols—four young Russian soldiers on horseback, "machine guns under their arms. When they reached the fences," he observed, "they paused to look, and, with a brief, timid exchange of words, turned their gazes ... to the jumbled pile of corpses, to the ruined barracks, and to ... [the] few living beings."

> They didn't smile; they appeared oppressed, not only by pity but by a confused restraint, which sealed their mouths, and riveted their eyes to the mournful scene. It was a shame well-known to us, the shame that inundated us after the selections and every time we had to witness or submit to an outrage: the shame that the Germans didn't know, and which the just man feels before a sin committed by another. It troubles him that it exists, that it has been irrevocably introduced into the world of things that exist, and that his good will availed nothing, or little, and was powerless to defend against it.[64]

* * *

With materials so dreadful, so without historical precedent, Levi needed to be exact in recall and description. At the same time, it was *his* recollection, and he had to be there in the text. But the very terribleness of his story required an emotional reserve, a reserve that eschewed all excess, a reserve that avoided self-pity—a reserve that bordered on self-effacement.

Henri testifies

"Henri" turned up as one of Levi's "saved." Levi wrote: he "is only twenty-two"—in fact he was seventeen—"is eminently civilized and sane, ... is extremely intelligent, speaks French, German, English, and Russian":

> Henri has ... [a] delicate and subtly androgynous body ...: his eyes are dark and profound, he has no beard yet, he moves with a natural languid elegance ... [He] is perfectly aware of his gifts and exploits them with the cool competence of someone handling a scientific instrument....
>
> Like the ichneumon wasp that paralyzes a large hairy caterpillar, wounding it in its sole vulnerable ganglion, Henri sizes up the subject, *son type*, at a glance. He speaks to him briefly, in the appropriate language, and the *type* is conquered: he listens with increasing sympathy, he is moved by the fate of this unfortunate young man, and it isn't long before he begins to yield returns....
>
> To speak with Henri is useful and pleasant. Sometimes one feels a warmth and closeness; communication, even affection, appears possible. One seems to glimpse the sorrowful, conscious human depths of his uncommon personality. But the next moment his sad smile freezes into a cold grimace that appears practiced at the mirror. Henri politely excuses himself... and here he is again, intent on his hunt and his struggle: hard and distant, enclosed in armor, the enemy of all, sly and incomprehensible, like the Serpent in Genesis.[65]

Levi knew that Henri—his real name was Paul Steinberg—came through the war; but he had no wish to contact him.

Steinberg had survived the evacuation from Auschwitz, the march to Gleiwitz, the three-day journey in an open car—"you had to climb up the slatted sides and tumble over the top"—along with between 100 and 120 other prisoners, a journey that ended in Buchenwald.[66] When the war was over, he returned to Paris, pursued a business career, and raised a family. And five decades later, ten years following Levi's death and shortly before his own, he published a memoir, *Speak You Also*—a memoir marked by a strange jokiness, a self-deprecatory irony, and mordant wit.

* * *

"I don't believe in the steadfast hero," Steinberg commented, "who endures every trial with his head held high, the tough guy who never gives in. Not in Auschwitz. If such a man exists, I never met him, and it must be hard for him to sleep with that halo." Auschwitz, he remarked, produced "a different variety of human being, no longer *Homo sapiens* but 'extermination-camp man.'" He pictured himself as one of the few who, with "the flexibility of a contortionist," managed to adapt.[67]

Looking back on his childhood, Steinberg claimed, he realized that he had had "the advantage of an intensive and extensive preparation for life in a concentration camp. A kind of immersion course. It's all there: the continual displacements and readjustments, the absence of ties ..., a hostile environment. Unable to rely on any outside support," he was "trained for solitary combat."[68]

The facts are these: the youngest of three children, born in Berlin in late 1926 to Russian émigrés—his mother died in childbirth; from age seven on, "bundled around from country to country ...—that is to say, Berlin, San Remo, Juan-les-Pins, Paris, Barcelona," and, once more, Paris; "ten years' worth of disruptions." Back in the French capital the family "played musical apartments" until they alighted in Auteuil; Steinberg "waltzed" from school to school until he entered seventh grade at Lycée Claude-Bernard. He now found himself "caught between two worlds." Home: "the closed universe of Russian refugees." They ate "lots of borscht, croquettes Pozharsky, kasha, cucumbers Malassol, and herring blinis, with caviar on special occasions." School: friends, their parents, sports, studies—very little of the latter. He was a "natural goof-off," working only when he wanted to or when he liked the teacher. But languages he knew: "German was ... [his] mother tongue, so to speak," and French his "vernacular," while English was the language he had spoken with his much older brother and "studied successfully in school. Finally, Russian was the rule with ... father, sister," and (hated) stepmother—he was "literally at home in it."[69]

How did Steinberg come to acquire a knowledge of chemistry, enough to get him work in a laboratory? At Claude-Bernard, he had had a physics and chemistry teacher who, "by some miracle, through some improbable channel," had "managed to get him interested in chemistry." Only chemistry, he was "a washout in physics."[70] En route to Auschwitz, Steinberg had a chance for further study.

It was not until September 1943 that Steinberg was arrested. Obsessed with gambling, he had spent the previous summer at the race track—having long ago stopped wearing the mandatory yellow star. Not so obsessed that he failed to pay attention to the news. He had noticed his "circle gradually thinning"; he had "heard about the Vél d'hiv roundups"—in July 1942 French police arrested 13,000 Jews in Paris, interning them, under appalling conditions, in the Vélodrome d'hiver sports arena before shipping them to Auschwitz. He had tried to go into hiding, but the people he approached refused to run the risk. On September 23, two plainclothes policemen caught up with him— "the informer's letter" having been "quite explicit."

> Times were hard: the police didn't have a car so we took the Métro. They explained to me that they were armed and would use their guns if I tried to escape. They didn't bother with handcuffs ... We got out at Odéon and I had a strange inspiration. I asked my cops if I could duck into Librairie Maloine, a bookstore on rue de l'École-de-Médecine: I still had a tiny reserve left over from my exploits at the track, and I chose a book of analytical inorganic chemistry ... The book was to come with me to Drancy, the collection camp on the northeastern outskirts of Paris, and on to Auschwitz, where it was confiscated, but by then I knew it by heart.[71]

Eight months after his arrival in Buna (more about those eight months shortly), Steinberg, like Levi, appeared before Dr. Pannwitz to take an oral exam.

> He asked me my age. "Eighteen," I said, stretching it a bit. "What have you studied?" I was off and running. A speech prepared in advance and rehearsed twenty times. I told him that I'd been the youngest in my year to pass the baccalauréat exam, that I was crazy about chemistry, that I'd also taken the entrance exam at the Institut de Chimie de Paris on rue Pierre-Curie, that I'd passed on the first try with an outstanding grade in chemistry, an average grade in math, and a mediocre one in physics (to make everything seem more plausible) ....
> He looked at me doubtfully and said, "Well, let's see, you're good in analytic chemistry. Tell me something about the chemistry of chromium." I closed my eyes and distinctly saw the page on chromium in the holy book. As clear as a photo. I calmly reeled off the series of reagents and precipitates from A to Z....
> He raised his glasses slightly and I had the feeling that I'd done it. "That's fine," he told me, "you can go."[72]

As it turned out, Steinberg did not start to work in a laboratory until weeks before the evacuation. (He remembered being in the same laboratory as Levi, "but this is certainly wrong. From his descriptions it is clear that he was in the Styrene laboratory."[73])

* * *

Levi encountered Steinberg sometime in the summer of 1944. The younger man had been in Buna since the previous October. He had entered the camp along with 340 other men; within three months that number had been whittled down by 40 percent; within eight months, by 60 percent; within a year, by 85 percent. The evacuation of Auschwitz reduced the remaining 15 percent to a handful of survivors.[74]

A series of illnesses had nearly done Steinberg in—and had also saved his life. (His closest friend, Philippe, succumbed. Steinberg saw him "melting away like an ice cube.") First, wounds in his leg, which later became ulcers— the result of a Kapo's barrage of kicks. Second, hepatitis—his "bad luck" during the tattooing. Someone whose last name began with R had the hepatitis virus. Steinberg, along with thirty or forty others, was infected, and may have been the only one to recover. Third, scabies, caught from his bunkmate. The itching invaded his whole body, and at night he would scratch himself bloody, without realizing it. Fourth, dysentery. "How many times," he wondered, did he make the trip back to camp with his "right hand jammed" between his "buttocks to keep the diarrhea that was slowly draining" him from soaking through his trousers and running down his legs into his clogs. "At the camp entrance, you had to march in time with the band, eyes right and sphincter tight." Then, finally, erysipelas. He reckoned that he "must have reached the same point as Philippe before ... his death." He could see "reflected in other people's eyes the image of a *Muselmann* in the making. A *Muselmann* whose time was running out."[75]

Saved his life—how? After a sulfa drug, of which there was only a limited supply, proved effective in curing his erysipelas, his "doctor pals" decided to stash him in the convalescents' block. ("A sumptuous aberration, ... a small island of peace," permitted by the SS on condition of frequent selections.) Thanks to his month-long stay, he "slowly regained strength and changed categories"—from pre-Muselmann to "acceptable Häftling."[76]

As Levi saw it, Steinberg's "free entry" into the infirmary stood as the clearest example of his talent for managing people. ("His friends ... admit him whenever he wants and with the diagnosis he wants. This takes place above all immediately before selections, and in periods of the heaviest work: to 'hibernate,' as he says."[77]) For his part, Steinberg claimed "to have practiced all the professions of the circus: lion tamer, tightrope walker, even magician." So it had been in dealing with the senior camp inmate.

> A French forced laborer agreed to mail a letter for me, and, stupefaction, six weeks later I received a small package of not more than two pounds, opened and partially pillaged … Still, I found sugar cubes, a tin of sardines, cookies, and a wrapper of a Meunier chocolate bar. I thought long and hard and decided to invest my goods productively.
>
> I visited the *Lagerältester* [senior camp inmate]; I told him that I'd received a little parcel and that … I wished to share my windfall with him. I was perfectly aware that I was behaving like a whore, and at the same time, I felt like a tamer of wild beasts entering the tiger's cage armed with a chair and a slab of gamy meat.
>
> I stroked the tiger's whiskers.
>
> I suppose I must have surprised him silly … He protested like a flustered virgin, a two-hundred pound virgin, then accepted the tin of sardines, not without insisting that I take a sausage in return. That proved to be the most profitable investment I ever made in my life, paying splendid dividends.
>
> I concluded that each one of the monsters had a flaw, a weakness, which it was up to me to find: this one needed flattering, that one had a repressed paternal instinct or the need to confide in someone who seemed to take an interest in him.
>
> Still others—and you had to watch out for them—loved young flesh and were on the lookout for a sex object. The camp was a gigantic market of homosexuality. All these criminals, idle and well fed, were deprived of women and fantasized nonstop.[78]

Steinberg denied that he had ever had sexual relations with another man—his demurral is not altogether convincing. Of course, what took place in the camps says nothing about same-sex intimacy and everything about sexual power. Steinberg skirted this issue—the one false note in his unsparing self-assessment.

* * *

October 1944. Steinberg has been in Buna for a year. He considers himself "a veteran, smartly dressed according to the local fashion," and is considered "an influential man, … said to have powerful protectors." In the barrack he has a bed all to himself "near the elite section" where the senior block inmate has his quarters. He has been asked "to lend a hand in the mornings and evenings to help keep order"—making him an honorary barrack-room attendant. Which brings him "certain material advantages and some self-satisfaction."

> Early one morning I inspect the row of beds in my charge to see that they are properly made and find myself nose to nose with an old man who's still lying in the middle bunk. He's a Polish Jew at the end of his road ... I tell him to hop out of there and make his bed. When he looks at me and mumbles in Yiddish, I get the impression he's defying me.
>
> Furious, I raise my hand without thinking and slap him. In the last moment, I hold back and my hand just grazes his cheek....
>
> I see his eyes ... Eyes without tears or reproaches. Just a blink in expectation of a slap from a hand. My hand.[79]

That incident, Steinberg wrote, haunted him. "The contagion had done its job," he had taken his "proper place ... in that world of violence."[80]

* * *

Levi's indictment of him casts a long shadow across the pages of Steinberg's book:

> How strange it is to see oneself at a distance of fifty years through the eyes of a neutral and surely objective observer ... He paints a picture of a rather unlikeable fellow, something of a cold fish, whom he found pleasant, it's true, but never wanted to see again....
>
> I was surely like that, ferociously determined to do anything to live, ready to use all means at hand, including a gift for inspiring sympathy and pity.
>
> The strangest thing about this acquaintance that seems to have left such precise traces in ... [Levi's] memory is that I do not remember him at all. Perhaps because I hadn't felt that he could be useful to me? Which would confirm his judgment.

Now, Steinberg added, with "a strong sense of regret, ... Primo Levi is gone ... Maybe I could have persuaded him to change his verdict by showing that there were extenuating circumstances."[81]

Coda

In chapter 11, Levi recounted a conversation, a conversation that had the flavor of a dream report, the manifest content of which was a fragment from Canto

XXVI of Dante's *Inferno*, the so-called Canto of Ulysses. Dante's Ulysses is not Homer's—there is no evidence that Dante knew the *Odyssey*. In the *Inferno*, Ulysses stands as the archetypal journeyer, determined to venture where no man has dared to go. Thanks to his rhetorical talents, he convinces his crew to join him. After years of travel, they reach the Pillars of Hercules, understood to be the rim of the earth. And just as legend foretold, disaster awaits in the form of a whirlwind that sinks the ship.

The occasion for the conversation was this. Every day, around noontime, Jean, the Pikolo—the youngest man in the Kommando who served as messenger clerk to the Kapo—collected the soup ration from the kitchen. To carry the fifty-kilo load, supported on two poles, he needed assistance. On a warm June day, a day that made Levi think of a summer beach, Jean asked Levi to help him. They were already acquainted: during an allied bombing raid, they had found themselves alone in a little shelter and for twenty minutes they had talked about their studies, their families, their mothers.[82] Now they set out to fetch the ration—about a kilometer away. "Pikolo," Levi wrote, "was experienced. He had chosen the path cleverly, so that we could make a long circuit, walking for at least an hour, without arousing suspicion"—and unencumbered by a heavy pot. Jean, who was from Alsace and spoke French and German with equal facility, knew a smattering of Italian and was eager to learn more. Levi was keen to teach.

The Canto of Ulysses—who knows why—comes to Levi's mind. "Jean pays close attention ... [He] is intelligent, he will understand. He *will* understand." Levi explains who Dante is, what the *Divine Comedy* is, how the *Inferno* is divided up. Levi recalls lines, stops, tries to translate. "Disastrous—poor Dante and poor French! All the same, the experience seems to auger well." Then nothing, a hole in Levi's memory. Another line, another hole. A phrase: "*but I set out upon the open sea*."

> "Open sea," "open sea (*mare aperto*), I know it rhymes with "deserted" (*deserto*): "... and with that small company of those who never deserted me," but I no longer remember if it comes before or after. And the journey as well, the foolhardy journey beyond the Pillars of Hercules, how sad, I have to tell it in prose: a sacrilege ....
>
> The sun is already high, midday is near. I'm in a hurry, a terrible hurry. Here, listen Pikolo, open your ears and your mind, you have to understand for my sake:

Consider well the seed that gave you birth:

you were not made to live your lives as brutes,

but to be followers of worth and knowledge.

As if I, too, were hearing it for the first time: like the blast of a trumpet, like the voice of God. For a moment I forget who I am and where I am.

Pikolo begs me to repeat it … Perhaps, despite the feeble translation and the pedestrian, rushed commentary, he has received the message, he has understood that it has to do with him, … with us in particular; and that it has to do with us two, who dare to talk about these things with the soup poles on our shoulders. . . .

Other lines dance in my head: "The tearful earth gave forth a wind," no, it's something else. It's late, it's late, we've reached the kitchen, I have to finish:

Three times it turned her round with all the waters;

And at the fourth, it lifted up the stern

so that our prow plunged deep, as pleased an Other.

I hold Pikolo back, it is vitally necessary and urgent that he listen, that he understand … before it is too late; tomorrow he or I might be dead, or we might never see each other again. I must tell him, I must explain to him about the Middle Ages, … and something else, something gigantic that I myself have only just seen, in a flash of intuition, perhaps the reason for our fate, for our being here today.[83]

They take their places in the "soup line, among the sordid, ragged crowd of soup-carriers from other Kommandos."[84] Levi's recitation trails off: the intuition—the insight into the reason why—is stillborn.

4

"Naturally": Imre Kertész

On March 19, 1944, German forces took possession of Hungary. With the outcome of the war amply apparent, the Hungarian government, now eager to jettison its longtime ally, had established contact with the Western Powers. Hitler quite appropriately feared that the Hungarians aimed to emulate the Italians. (The Italians had signed an armistice with the Allies in September 1943; the Germans had responded by invading.) Occupation was again Hitler's answer—which, in turn, made possible the liquidation of Hungarian Jews.[1]

Anti-Semitism was nothing new in Hungary. In 1920, after the collapse of a short-lived Bolshevik regime and the consolidation of a semi-autocracy under Admiral Miklós Horthy, the so-called *numerus clausus* law, a law restricting the number of Jews admitted to institutions of higher education, was passed. Then in the late 1920s, the law's most discriminatory elements were repealed. For the better part of the following decade, that is, until 1938, when Nazi Germany, having gobbled up Austria, arrived at the Hungarian border, no new anti-Jewish legislation was enacted. Between 1938 and 1941, Hungary, thanks to German and Italian support, regained about 40 percent of the territories it had lost after the First World War and therewith saw the size of its Jewish population increase—reaching roughly 800,000. Anti-Semitism, on the part of the public and politicians alike, grew apace, prompting a long list of restrictions: on Jews in business and the professions, on marriages and extramarital sex between Jews and non-Jews. Nonetheless, before the German occupation, compared to Jews in other parts of Hitler's Europe, those in Hungary were living a normal life. A young Zionist leader, arriving in Budapest from Slovakia in January 1944, was astounded: "For me, ... this seemed like fantasy ... Jews seeking entertainment could still visit coffee houses, cinemas and theaters. While in Poland, hundreds of thousands of Europe's Jews were being annihilated."[2]

When the Wehrmacht occupied Hungary, Horthy stayed put and ordered the army not to resist. His decision to continue as regent played into the hands of the Nazis who were eager to maintain a façade of Hungarian sovereignty—the better to maximize German exploitation of Hungary's economic and military resources, the better to implement the Final Solution. To that end, a special commando squad of around 150 to 200 men, organized under the immediate command of Adolf Eichmann, accompanied the German troops. It was in Hungary that Eichmann, finally, had the chance to test his effectiveness in the field.

And he was able to proceed with lightning speed—owing to the enthusiastic assistance of the Hungarian government. Within days of Eichmann's arrival, it adopted a framework for the isolation and expropriation of the Jews. An initial decree required Jews to wear the Star of David, thus separating them from the Christian population; a second, addressed in confidence to the leading officials of the gendarmerie, police, and state administration, called for ghettoization and deportation. The techniques used adhered to Eichmann's master plan and were basically the same throughout the country. Jewish leaders in each community were ordered to provide lists of all Jews along with their addresses. In hamlets, villages, and smaller towns, the round-ups were carried out by the gendarmerie; in the larger cities, the police acted in concert with local civil servants. After a few weeks, the ghettoized Jews were transferred to deportation centers, usually in county seats. Each day three or four trains were scheduled to depart, with each train carrying approximately 3,000 Jews. To make sure that the extermination project ran without a hitch, the de-Jewification experts divided Hungary into six operational zones. In zone one, Carpatho-Ruthenia and northeastern Hungary, the mass deportation began at dawn on May 15. Less than two months later, deportations from the fifth zone, western Hungary and the suburbs of Budapest, were complete. The Hungarian and German agencies involved were scrupulous recordkeepers. On July 15, Edmund Veessenmayer, Hitler's plenipotentiary in Budapest, reported back to Berlin that 437,402 Jews had reached their destination—Auschwitz-Birkenau. Of these, roughly 25 percent were selected for labor; the rest were murdered on arrival.[3]

In anticipation of the 12,000 to 14,000 new arrivals each day, the extermination machinery was put into peak condition. To provide a direct link to the death factory, a new railway branch line—which was to become the iconic image of Auschwitz—was laid between Auschwitz and Birkenau. The crematoria were renovated: the furnaces were relined; the chimneys were strengthened with iron bands; pits were dug in the vicinity of the gas chambers to burn the corpses that were beyond the capacity of the crematoria. By the time the first transports appeared, the machinery of destruction was ready to ensure a regular, efficient, and continuous assembly-line operation on a scale never before achieved.

The provinces had been cleared of Jews; those in Budapest were next-up. On July 7, Horthy—having been deluged with protests from neutral countries, from the Vatican, and from the Allies, who drove home their disapproval by an unusually heavy air raid on Budapest—ordered the deportations to stop. Without the regent's consent and the collaboration of Hungarian authorities, Eichmann could not continue planning any large-scale operations. The Jews in the capital were no longer in immediate danger.

This state of relative calm lasted until October 15. Horthy openly— rather than covertly—tried to break with Berlin; the Germans thwarted his attempt, forced him to resign and to transfer power to Ferenc Szálasi, leader of the Hungarian facsimile of the Nazis, the Arrow Cross Party. Terror was unleashed against Jews in Budapest; deportations resumed as well. The Arrow Cross government herded—mostly by foot—a total of 50,000 people to the country's western border or to the Reich. Again protests by neutral countries had a telling effect. The Arrow Cross gradually stopped the death marches and began instead organizing ghettos in Budapest. Liberation came on the heels of the Red Army in January 1945.

At the age of fourteen, Imre Kertész, the son of a fairly well-off businessman, was among the 437,402 Jews sent to Birkenau—though he scarcely considered himself Jewish. Years later he commented: "My Jewishness is shaped by the Holocaust. I do not speak Hebrew, I did not have a religious education or upbringing, I am not familiar with Jewish philosophy, … I am not religious, I never was. Religion has never meant anything to me."[4] Kertész and people like him felt themselves to be Hungarians of the "Israelite persuasion," or, more often, of no religious persuasion whatsoever—even at a time when anti-Jewish laws followed one another, even at a time when a huge number of Hungarians could hardly wait to get rid of the Jews.

Kertész survived Birkenau; he survived Buchenwald, then Zeitz, then again Buchenwald. (He died in 2016.) At war's end he returned to a country now occupied by Soviet troops and where Communist influence soon became dominant. His father was dead, having succumbed in a concentration camp; the family apartment had been expropriated. Kertész needed to finish high school—often sitting next to students for whom the war had been a brief and exciting adventure in air-raid shelters. Later he tried his hand at many things, including a stint as a day laborer, journalism, writing librettos for musical comedies, and finally translating works by Nietzsche, Freud, Wittgenstein, and others into the Hungarian language. Looking back on those postwar years from the vantage point of 2002, from the vantage point of being awarded the Nobel Prize for Literature, he remarked: "If I ... size up honestly the situation I was in at the time, I have to conclude that in the West, in a free society, I probably would not have been able to write the novel known by readers today as ... [*Fatelessness*], the novel singled out by the Swedish Academy for the highest honor."[5]

That novel, published in 1975, took thirteen years to complete. Why did Kertész call it fiction? Critics commonly refer to *Fatelessness* as an autobiographical novel—and appropriately so. "Every facet of the story," he admitted, "is based on documented facts."[6] What is brilliant about his work, from the very first sentences, is its deceptive plainness and the meticulously reported detail. Here are those opening lines:

> I didn't go to school today. Or rather, I did go, but only to ask my class teacher's permission to take the day off. I also handed him a letter in which, referring to "family reasons," my father requested that I be excused. He asked what the "family reason" might be. I told him my father had been called up for labor service; after that he didn't raise a further peep against it.[7]

Readers will be more alarmed than Gyuri, the fourteen-year-old protagonist. In fact they are several steps ahead of him, feeling the pull of worry and dread. They, like the teacher, can detect the reality that lurks behind a polite formula like "family reasons" or a euphemism like "labor service." Kertész's narrative technique—ironic through and through—requires the reader to be more perceptive and informed than the protagonist.[8]

What is given in the text is Gyuri's vision of things. He is granted an extremely active mind, and that activity is devoted to interpreting what he sees and hears. It is assumed that he has no prior knowledge; he must figure things out firsthand for himself. He is caught, as Kertész put it, in "the dreary trap of linearity"[9]; he has to live through everything. No time shifts for Kertész. What is difficult or impossible to distinguish—as in the opening sentence, "I didn't go to school today"—is the language of the narrator *now*, in an unidentified present, from that of the protagonist, *then*, in the narrated past.[10]

Just what does the title—fatelessness—mean? At the end of the book, Gyrui, having returned to Budapest, meets up with two honorary uncles. In talking to them, he realizes all at once, and with a flash of clarity:

> I could no longer be satisfied with the notion that it had all been a mistake, ... some kind of blunder, let alone that it had not even happened ... I almost pleaded, that I could not swallow that idiotic bitterness, that I should merely be innocent ... It's about steps. Everyone took steps as long as he was able to take a step; I too took my own steps; and not just in the queue at Birkenau, but even before that, here, at home.[11]

Capturing the step-by-step movement through time, that alone makes it possible to take possession of one's history, one's fate.

* * *

In *If This Is a Man*, Primo Levi wrote of Muselmänner, the "anonymous mass ... of non-men who march and labor in silence ... One hesitates to call them living, one hesitates to call their death death—in the face of it they have no fear, because they are too tired to understand."[12] In *The Drowned and the Saved*, he elaborated: they, the Muselmänner, were the majority who touched bottom. They "did not come back to tell, or they came back mute ... Even if they had possessed pen and paper, ... [they] could not have borne witness because their death had already begun before the body perished. Weeks and months before dying, they had already lost the ability to observe, to remember, to measure, and to express themselves ... But it is they, ... the witnesses to everything—they are the ones whose testimony would have had a comprehensive meaning."[13]

In *Fatelessness*, Kertész tries to bear witness to something to which it is impossible to bear witness.[14]

"I ought to have been learning … about Auschwitz"

Two months have passed since Gyuri's father was called up for labor service. The boy is no longer in school. The students have been let out—owing, the authorities claim, to the ongoing war. Gyuri has been employed in a company in Csepel, the Shell Oil Refinery. "As a result," he has "actually acquired a privilege of sorts, since under other circumstances those wearing yellow stars are prohibited from traveling outside the city limits." He has been "handed legitimate papers, bearing the official stamp of the war production department," which allows him to "cross the Csepel customs borderline."[15]

"A slightly odd experience"—so Kertész begins the chapter in which he recounts Gyuri's arrest.

> I got up that morning and set off to work as usual. It promised to be a hot day, and as ever the bus was packed with passengers. We had already left the houses of the suburbs behind and driven across the short … bridge … to Csepel Island, … when the bus braked very suddenly, and then I heard from the outside snatches of a voice issuing orders, which the conductor and several passengers relayed down to me, to the effect that any Jewish passengers who happened to be on the bus should get off. I thought to myself, no doubt they want to do a spot-check on the papers of everyone going across.
>
> Indeed, on the highway I found myself face-to-face with a policeman. Without a word being said, I immediately held out my pass toward him. He, however, first sent the bus on its way with a brisk flip of the hand. I was beginning to think that maybe he didn't understand the ID, and was just on the point of explaining to him that, as he could see, I am assigned to war work, when all at once the road around me was thronged with voices and boys, my companions from Shell. They had emerged from … behind … [an] embankment. It turned out that the policeman had already grabbed them off earlier buses, and they were killing themselves with laughter that I too had turned up. Even the policeman cracked a bit of a smile …; I could see straightaway that he had nothing against us—nor indeed could he have had, actually.[16]

The day dragged on: a long wait for instructions. The boys—and also the adults, who trickled in and to whom the policeman was "less cordial"—settled down in the customs post. Around 4:00 the order came through. They were to make their way to a "higher authority" to show their documents. The policeman volunteered, though nothing specific had been communicated to him, that "in his view it could be no more than some kind of cursory formality, at least in cases that were as clearcut and incontestable in the eyes of the law as, for instance, ours were."

> Columns, drawn up in ranks of three abreast, set off back toward the city from all the border posts in the area simultaneously, as I was able to establish while we were en route … Finally, it hit me that I was marching in the middle of what was by now a sizable column, with our procession flanked on both sides, at sporadic intervals, by policemen.
>
> We proceeded in this manner, spread over the entire road, for quite a long while. It was a fine, clear, summery afternoon, the streets thronged with a motley multitude … I … lost my sense of bearings rather quickly, since we mostly traversed streets and avenues with which I was not … that familiar … All I remember of the entire long trek, in fact, was the kind of hasty, hesitant, almost furtive curiosity of the public on the sidewalks at the sight of our procession …—oh, and a subsequent, somewhat disturbing moment. We happened to be going along some broad, tremendously busy avenue in the suburbs, with the honking, unbearably noisy din of traffic all around us, when at one point, I don't know how, a streetcar managed to become wedged in our column, not far in front of me as it happened. We were obliged to come to a halt while it passed through, and it was then that I became alive to a sudden flash of yellow clothing up ahead, in the cloud of dust, noise, and vehicle exhaust fumes: it was "Traveler" [one of the boys]. A single long leap, and he was off to the side, lost somewhere in the seething eddy of machines and humanity … I saw one or two enterprising spirits then immediately make a break for it in his wake, right up ahead. I myself took a look around, though more for the fun of it, if I may put it that way, since I saw no other reason to bolt, though I believe there would have been time to do so; nevertheless, my sense of honor proved stronger. The policemen took immediate action after that, and the ranks again closed around me.[17]

After going on a while longer, they were led into "some sort of barracks parade ground." There a "tall figure of commanding presence" ordered that "the whole Jewish rabble" be taken off "to the place that, in his view, they actually belonged—the stables, that is to say." Gyuri, bewildered by the "immediately ensuing indecipherable babble of commands, the bellowed orders, ... didn't know which way ... to turn." He "felt a bit like laughing, in part out of astonishment and confusion, a sense of having been dropped slap in the middle of some crazy play," in which he was not "acquainted" with his role.[18]

* * *

Everything became "clear only gradually, sequentially ... step-by-step." And by the time Gyuri had "passed a given step," put it behind him, the next one was already there.[19]

Within days, he and his pals were on their way to Auschwitz-Birkenau. They had no inkling of their destination. They had been told "that anyone inclined to do so could present himself for work" in the Reich. They had also been told that "the consignment would have to be made up one way of another," and insofar as the lists fell short, they would have no choice in the matter. Gyuri actually found the idea of going to Germany "attractive."[20]

Why attractive? What did Gyuri know of the Germans?

> Many people, particularly the older ones with experience to look back on, professed that whatever ideas they might have about the Jews, the Germans were fundamentally, as everybody knew, tidy, honest, industrious people with a fondness for order and punctuality who appreciated the same traits in others, which did indeed, by and large, roughly correspond with what I myself knew about them, and it occurred to me that no doubt I might also derive some benefit from having acquired some fluency in their language at grammar school. What I could look forward to from working ... was above all orderliness, employment, new impressions, and a bit of fun—all in all, a more sensible lifestyle more to my liking than the one here in Hungary, just as ... we boys, quite naturally, pictured it when we talked among ourselves.[21]

And so they were sent packing—in a freight train made up of brick red boxcars with locked doors.

On the morning of the fourth day, Gyuri was awakened by "a bustling and flurry of excitement." A minute later, the train "slipped under the arch of some form of gateway." Another minute passed, the train came to a halt. From outside, noise, a "banging, a clattering-back of doors, the commingling hubbub of passengers swarming from the train." Next a tool snapped on the door of Gyuri's car, and "somebody, or rather several somebodies rolled the heavy door aside."

I heard their voices first. They spoke German or some language close to that ... As far as I could make out, they wanted us to get off at once. Instead, though, it seemed they were pushing their way up among us ... Then they got closer to me in the hurley-burley, and I finally got my first glimpse of the people here. It was quite a shock, for after all, this was the first time in my life that I had seen, up close at any rate, real convicts, in the striped duds of criminals, and with shaven skulls in round caps ... On the chest of each one, apart from the customary convict's number, I also saw a yellow triangle ... Their faces did not exactly inspire confidence ...: jug ears, prominent noses, sunken, beady eyes with a crafty gleam. Quite like Jews in every respect. I found them suspect and altogether foreign-looking. When they spotted us boys, I noticed, they became quite agitated. They immediately launched into a hurried, somehow frantic whispering, which was when I made the surprising discovery that Jews evidently don't speak only Hebrew, as I had supposed up till now: "*Rays di yiddish, rayds di yiddish, rayds di yiddish*?" ["Do you speak Yiddish?"] was what they were asking. "*Nein,*" we told them, the boys and me too ... Then suddenly on the basis of my German, I found it easy to figure out—they all started to get very curious about our ages. We told them, "*Vierzehn*" or "*Fünfzehn,*" depending on how old each of us was. They immediately raised a huge protestation, with hands, heads, their entire bodies: "*Zestsayn!*" they muttered left, right, and center, "*zestsayn.*" I was surprised and even asked one of them: "*Warum?*" "*Willst du arbeiten?*"—Did I want to work, he asked ... "*Natürlich,*" I told him, since that was my reason for coming, if I thought about it. At this, he not only grabbed me by the arm with a tough, bony, yellow hand but gave it a good shake, saying then in that case "*Zestsayn! ... vershtayst di? Zestsayn!*" I could see he was exasperated, on top of which the thing, as I saw it, was obviously very important for him, and since we boys had by then swiftly conferred on this, I somewhat cheerfully agreed: all right, I'll be sixteen, then.

Gyuri edged his way to the door and took a "big leap out into the daylight."[22]

A long column formed, "made up solely of men, all in regularly ordered ranks of five" and moved forward steadily. Up ahead a bath awaited, but first a "medical inspection" was in store for all the new arrivals. At one point "the rows of five transformed into a single file"; at the same time, they were told to remove their jackets and shirts, so as to present themselves stripped to the waist. The pace "was also quickening."

The inspection itself could only have required around two or three seconds … The doctor … took a … [close] look as me with a studied, serious and attentive glance … I was able to get a good look at him while he, resting his gloved hands on my cheeks, pried my lower eyelids down a bit on both sides with his thumbs in an action I was familiar with from doctors back home. As he was doing that, in a quiet yet very distinct tone that revealed him to be a cultured man, he asked, though almost as if it were of secondary importance, "*Wie alt bist du?*" "*Sechszehn*" ["How old are you?" "Sixteen."] I told him. He nodded perfunctorily, but somehow more at this being the appropriate response … rather than the truth—at least that was my impression offhand … I sensed that he must have taken a shine to me. Then, still pushing against my cheek with one hand while indicating the direction with the other, he dispatched me to the far side of the path … The boys were waiting there, exultant, chortling gleefully. At the sight of those beaming faces, I also understood, perhaps, what it was that distinguished our group from the bunch across on the opposite side: it was success, if I sensed correctly.[23]

By the end of the first day, Gyuri understood just about everything: that "there across the way, at that very moment, fellow passengers … were burning— all those … who up in front of the doctor had proved unfit due to old age or other reasons, along with little ones and the mothers who were with them and expectant women"; that "they too had proceeded from the station to the baths"; that "they too had been informed about the hooks, the numbers, and the washing procedure, just the same" as Gyuri and his friends. "The barbers were also there, so it was alleged, and the bars of soap were handed out in just the same way. Then they too had entered the bathroom itself, with the same pipes and showerheads, … only out of these came, not water, but gas."

It all somehow roused in me a sense of certain jokes, a kind of student prank … Of course, I was well aware that it was not altogether a joke …; nevertheless that was my impression, and fundamentally—or at least so I imagined—that must have been pretty much the way it happened. After all, people would have to meet to discuss this, put their heads together so to say, even if they were not exactly students but mature adults, quite possibly—indeed, in all likelihood—gentlemen in imposing suits, decorations on their chests, cigars in their mouths, presumably all in high command, who were not to be disturbed right then—that is how I imagined it. One of them comes up with the gas, another immediately follows with the bathhouse, a third with the soap, ... and so on. Some of the ideas may have provoked more prolonged discussion and amendment, whereas others would have been immediately hailed with delight, the men jumping up (I don't know why, but I insisted on their jumping up) and slapping one another's palms—this was all too readily imaginable, at least as far as I was concerned. By dint of many zealous hands and much toing and froing, the commanders' fantasy then becomes reality, and as I had witnessed, there was no room for doubt about the stunt's success.[24]

Something else impressed Gyuri: that Auschwitz had been in existence for a long time. He heard that the senior block inmate had been living there for four years. Four years, that meant Auschwitz was in operation when Gyuri entered grammar school. He recalled the ceremony for the start of the academic year.

> I too was there in a dark blue, braided Hungarian-style uniform ... Even the headmaster's words had registered, he himself being a man of distinguished and, now that I think back on it, of somewhat commanding presence, with severe eyeglasses and a majestic white handlebar moustache. In winding up he made reference, I recollected, to an ancient Roman philosopher, quoting the tag *"non scolae sed vitae discimus"*—"we learn for life, not school." But then in light of that, really, I ought to have been learning all along exclusively about Auschwitz ... Over the four years at school I had not heard a single word about it ... Now I would have to be edified here.[25]

An example: a *Vernichtungslager*, an extermination camp, was different from a *Konzentrationslager*, a concentration camp. The former was a pure killing center, the latter maintained a substantial prisoner and slave population. (Auschwitz-Birkenau was both.) And by the evening of the fourth day, Gyuri found himself again in one of those now familiar freight cars. The destination: Buchenwald, a concentration camp even older than Auschwitz.

"I would like to live a little longer"

Gyuri was in Buchenwald very briefly—long enough to be entered into the books. After the usual greeting—"bathhouse, barbers, disinfectant, and a change of clothes"—a fellow prisoner, "a long-term resident with hair," recorded Gyuri's name in a big register and handed him both a yellow triangle, in the middle of which was the letter U for Hungarian, and also a strip of linen cloth with a printed number, 64921. In Buchenwald they did not inscribe the number in a prisoner's skin. "And if you were … worried on that score and had inquired about it beforehand, in the bathhouse area, the old prisoner would raise his hands and, rolling his eyes to the ceiling in protest, [would] say: "*Aber Mensch, um Gotteswillen, wir sind doch hier nicht in Auschwitz!*" ("For God's sake, man, this isn't Auschwitz.")[26]

Zeitz, Gyuri's next destination, was also no Auschwitz; nor was it Buchenwald. It was "no more than some kind of small, mediocre, out-of-the-way, … rural concentration camp."[27] In 1944, satellite camps housed the bulk of the new prisoners, and by the following January, the number of such camps was well over 500.[28] As Gyuri saw it, "in any place, even a concentration camp," one starts out "with good intentions …; for the time being, it was sufficient to become a good prisoner, the rest was in the hands of the future."[29]

* * *

In Zeitz, on the first day, Gyuri met Bandi Citrom. (His pals had been sent elsewhere. Of the seventeen boys taken off the bus with Kertész, he was the only one to survive.[30]) Bandi had been conscripted as soon as Hungary entered the war in 1941. And because Jews were not allowed to bear arms, he had been deployed for mine-clearing in Ukraine, in a "punishment company … It took a spade, a length of wire, plus sheer pluck"—that was all he would vouchsafe about the work. Bandi tried to take Gyuri in hand, to instill, if not pluck, then some prudence into him. The main thing, Bandi insisted, "was not to neglect oneself."

> Under all circumstances … [one must] wash oneself (before parallel rows of troughs with the perforated iron piping, in the open air …). Equally essential was a frugal apportioning of the rations, whether or not there were any. Whatever rigor this disciplining might cost you, a portion of the bread ration had to be left for the next morning's coffee, some of it indeed—by maintaining an undeflectable guard against the inclination of your every thought, and above all of your itching fingers, to stray toward your pocket— for the lunch break: that way, and only that way, could you avoid … the tormenting thought, you had nothing to eat … That the only secure place to be at roll call and in a marching column was always the middle of a row; that even when soup was being dished out one would do better to aim, not for

the front, but the back of the queue, where you could predict they would be serving from the bottom of the vat, and therefore from the thicker sediment; that one side of the handle of your spoon could be hammered out into a tool that might also serve as a knife—all these things, and much else besides, all of it knowledge essential to prison life, I was taught by Bandi Citrom.[31]

Initially—during a period that Gyuri and Bandi later dubbed "the golden days"—"Zeitz, along with the conduct it required and a dash of luck, proved a very tolerable place." The prisoners, at the disposition of the Braun-Kohl-Benzin Aktiengesellschaft (Lignite Petroleum Company), were assigned to a variety of commandos—spades, pitchforks, cable-laying, cement-mixers among others. Gyuri soon learns to put the minimum of effort into handling a spade, shovel, or pitchfork, and to take the maximum number of breathers. He makes, at least as he judged it, "very considerable progress in such tactics, ... gaining a great deal" of expertise. Then, at day's end, the announcement to fall in signals the time to return to camp. Bandi squeezes through the throng around the washbasins with a shout, "Move over, Muslims!" and no part of Gyuri's body "can be kept hidden from his scrutiny. 'Wash your pecker too! That's where lice lodge,' he'll say," and Gyuri complies "with a laugh."[32]

The golden days did not last. Before long Gyuri's "zest dwindled," his "drive dwindled." Every day he found it a little bit harder to get up; every day he went to bed a little bit wearier; he was a little bit hungrier; it took him a little more effort to walk. Gyuri was "becoming a burden" even to himself. And then he caught a glimpse of his body.

I would never have believed ... that I could become a decrepit old man so quickly. Back home that takes time, fifty or sixty years at least; here three months was enough ... [My] skin was drooping in loose folds, jaundiced and desiccated, covered in all kinds of boils, brown rings, cracks, fissures, pocks, and scales that itched uncomfortably, especially between my fingers. "Scabies," Bandi ... diagnosed with a knowing nod of the head when I showed him ... Every day there was something new to surprise me, some new blemish, some new unsightliness on this ever stranger, ever more foreign object that had once been my good friend: my body ... I could no longer bear looking at it without a sense of being at war with myself ...; after a while, I no longer cared to strip off to have a wash.

Gyuri started to let himself go, and Bandi started to worry.

I became conscious of this one evening when he took me with him to the washroom. My flailing and protests were to no avail as he stripped me of my clothes with all the strength he could muster; my attempts to pummel his body and his face [were] to no avail as he scrubbed cold water over my shivering skin. I told him a hundred times over that his guardianship was a nuisance to me, he should leave me alone, just … [fuck] off. Did I want to croak right here, did I maybe not want to get back home, he asked, and I have no clue what answer he must have read from my face but, all at once, I saw some form of consternation or alarm written all over his, in much the same way as people generally view … condemned men or, let's say, carriers of pestilence, which was when the opinion he had once expressed about Muslims crossed my mind. In any event, from then on, he tended to steer clear of me.

All the same, Gyuri began to find "peace, tranquility, and relief."

Thus, if I grew tired while standing at *Appell* [roll-call], for example, without so much as a look at whether it was muddy or there was a puddle, I would simply take a seat, plop down, and stay down, until my neighbors forcibly pulled me up. Cold, damp, wind, or rain were no longer able to bother me … Even my hunger passed; I continued to carry to my mouth anything edible I was able to lay my hands on, but more out of absentmindedness, mechanically out of habit, so to say. As for work, I no longer strove to give the appearance of it. If people did not like that, at most they would beat me, and even then they could not truly do much harm, since for me it just won some time; at the first blow I would promptly stretch out on the ground and would feel nothing after that, since I would meanwhile drop off to sleep.[33]

Bandi performed one further service: Gyuri's right knee had been transformed into a "flaming red sac" and was extremely painful, too painful for him to make it to the infirmary willingly—and his knowledge of the place "did not exactly boost" his "confidence." So Bandi and a bunkmate, "forming a cradle of their hands, a bit like storks are said to carry their young to safety," deposited him at the spot.[34]

Gyuro never saw Bandi again. At the war's end, when he sought him out in Budapest, he learned that he had not survived.

* * *

From the infirmary, Gyuri was transferred—tossed into a truck—to the newly constructed hospital in Zeitz. A boy, roughly Gyuri's age, was dumped into the bunk beside him.

The sallow face and large, burning eyes seemed vaguely familiar to me, but then, equally, everyone here had a sallow face and large, burning eyes … I suspect he must have had a fever as heat was pouring steadily from his persistently shivering body, from which I was able to take agreeable profit. I was less enchanted with all his tossing and turning during the night … I told him as well: Hey! Cut it out, ease up there, and in the end he heeded the advice. I only saw why the next morning, when my repeated attempts to rouse him for coffee were futile. All the same, I hastily passed his mess tin to the orderly along with my own, since, just as I was about to report the case, he snappily asked me for it. I later also accepted his bread ration on his behalf, and likewise his soup that evening and so on for a while, until … he began to go really strange, which was when I felt obliged finally to say something, as I could not carry on stowing him in my bed after all … He was taken away … and nothing was said.

A "now familiar flaming red sac" appeared on Gyuri's left hip. An incision was made to drain the pus, and it was protected with a paper bandage. Plagued by a tickling sensation, Gyuri lifted the covering and discovered vermin "feeding on the wound."

I tried to snatch them away, get rid of them, at least root and winkle them out, compel them to wait and be patient at least a little bit longer, but I have to admit that never before had I sensed a more hopeless struggle or a more stubborn, even, so to say, more brazen resistance than this. After a while, indeed, I gave up and just watched the gluttony, the teeming, the voracity, the appetite, the unconcealed happiness … In the end, … even my sense of revulsion very nearly passed … I quickly covered the wound up and subsequently no longer engaged in combat with them, no longer disturbed them.[35]

Then the journey in the freight car back to Buchenwald. Gyuri, along with the others who were of no further use, was being "returned to sender as it were … Lying there … on the cold straw … dampened by all sorts of dubious fluids," his paper bandages, "long since frayed, peeled and … detached," his shirt and trousers pasted to his naked wounds, he was "almost lost in reverie." So too, when the icy floorboards of the train were replaced by puddles on paved ground. He just mused on one thing or another, looked fixedly at whatever happened to strike his eye "without any superfluous movement or effort."

Some time later, and I don't know if it was an hour, a day, or a year, I finally picked out voices, noises, the sounds of work, and tidying up. All of a sudden, the head next to me rose, and lower down, by the shoulders, I saw arms in prison garb preparing to toss it onto the top of a heap of other bodies that had already been piled on some kind of handcart ... At the same time, a snatch of speech that I was barely able to make out came to my attention ...: "I p ... pro ... test," it muttered ... I immediately heard another voice— obviously that of the person grasping him by the shoulders. "*Was? Du willst doch leben?*" ("What? You still want to live?")[36]

Gyuri also considered it odd, "since it could not be warranted." Yet when a man in prison clothes leaned over him, he, too, protested, not verbally; rather, he blinked. As a consequence of the fluttering eyelids, Gyuri was loaded onto a smaller handcart and pushed—he didn't know where.

A familiar-sounding clatter drifted up faintly my way from somewhere, like bells in dreams, and as I gazed down across the scene, I caught sight of a procession of bearers, poles on shoulders, groaning under the weight of steaming cauldrons, and from far off I recognized, there could be no doubting it, a whiff of turnip soup in the acrid air. A pity, because it must have been that spectacle, that aroma, which cut through my numbness to trigger an emotion, the growing waves of which were able to squeeze, even from my dried-out eyes, a few warmer drops amid the dankness that was soaking my face. Despite all deliberation, sense, insight, and sober reason, I could not fail to recognize within myself the furtive and yet—ashamed as it might be, so to say, of its irrationality—increasingly insistent voice of some muffled craving of sorts: I would like to live a little bit longer.[37]

* * *

Gyuri finds himself in a "strange place. Doors open off the corridor, real, proper, white-painted doors," behind one of which is a warm, bright room, and in there is a bed already empty and made-up, waiting for him.

The Pfleger [medical orderly] ... sits down on the edge of your bed, some sort of card and pencil in his hand, and asks you your name. "*Vier-und-sechzig, neun, ein-und-zwanzig*" [64921] I told him. He writes that down but keeps pushing, for it may take a while before you understand that he wants to know your name, "*Name,*" and then a further while ... before, after some rooting around in your memories, you hit upon it. He made me repeat it three or even four times until he finally seemed to understand. He then showed me what he had written, and at the top of some sort of ruled fever chart, I read: "*Keviszterz.*"[38]

Why has Gyuri landed in this strange place? The question perplexes him. If he takes a "rational view of things," he can see "no reason" why he should be in this hospital instead of somewhere else. When he thinks back to the series of events that brought him from the handcart to this room, this bed, he can hit upon no adequate explanation. Over time, and as he begins to mend, he comes to the conclusion that "one can become accustomed even to miracles."[39]

The medical orderly and the doctor, the visitors who popped in for a minute or two always at the same time in the evening—all of them wore red triangles, the mark of a political prisoner. Gyuri did not see a single green (denoting a criminal) or black triangle (denoting an asocial), nor, for that matter, a yellow one. From the letters on the triangles, he picked out Poles, the most numerous, and French, Czechs, Russians, Yugoslavs as well. By "race, language, and age," these prisoners were different from any Gyuri had ever known.[40]

From his bed, Gyuri registered the changes taking place in the camp. Looking at whatever there was to see, listening to the commands coming over the loudspeaker, he picked up comings and goings, "impending … inconveniences, disturbances, worries, and troubles." For example: repeated announcements, "*Frizeure zum Bad*" ("barbers to the bathhouse"), coupled with "*Leichenkommando zum Tor*" ("corpse-bearers to the gate") allowed him to judge the nature of the transports.[41] (Fourteen thousand prisoners from Auschwitz arrived in Buchenwald—Paul Steinberg was one of them.[42]) Gyuri had no idea when the barbers got any sleep; he heard that the newcomers "may have to stand around naked for two or three days in front of the bathhouse before being able to proceed further, while the *Leichenkommando*" was "constantly at work on its rounds."[43]

Will Gyuri be evacuated? Coming from the loudspeaker, he heard: "*Alle Juden im Lager*" (all Jews in the camp) "*sofort*" (immediately) "*antreten*" (to fall in). He sat up in bed, terrified, but Pyetchka, the orderly, "just smiled in his usual manner and gestured with both hands to lie back down, take it easy, no need to get worked up, what's the hurry."[44] (The camp SS forced some 28,000 prisoners out of the main camp; another 20,000 were left inside.[45])

Now Pyetchka himself was away for a prolonged interval, and when he returned, he carried a bundle wrapped in a sheet. It had a handle, and "from the middle … poked the tip of an implement" Gyuri "had never previously seen in a prisoner's hands, … an object that Pyetchka, before putting it under his bed," allowed the entire room "to see for a fleeting moment." It was a sawn-off shotgun. (How he had gotten hold of it remained a mystery.) Then, one morning, "not long after coffee, there were hurried footsteps in the corridor, a strident call, a code word as it were, at which Pyetchka swiftly scrabbled his package out from … its hiding place and, gripping it under his arm," vanished. Shortly thereafter, Gyuri heard, over the loudspeaker, "an instruction that was not for prisoners but [for] soldiers: '*An alle SS Angehörigen*,' then twice over, '*Das Lager sofort zu verlassen*,' ordering the forces to leave the camp at once."[46] (By afternoon, members of the camp defense formations had cut the barbed wire, occupied the watchtowers, and hoisted a white flag. "Thus the first American tanks, rumbling up from the northeast, found a Buchenwald that had already been liberated."[47])

Around 4:00, Gyuri heard the senior camp inmate announce "'*wir sind frei*,'—we are free … He proceeded to deliver a decent little speech; … after him, it was the turn of others" speaking in the most diverse languages. Then to Gyuri's "utter amazement, all of a sudden: … 'Attention, this is the Hungarian camp committee.'" He had "never even suspected there was such a thing." Gyuri kept hearing about freedom. He was "quite naturally … absolutely delighted"; but he couldn't help fretting about his soup—or lack thereof. For all his waiting throughout the day, "straining of ears, keeping eyes peeled and on the lookout, neither at the regular time nor later," did he manage "to pick out the … long-overdue rattling and the attendant daily hollering of the soup-bearers."

The April evening outside was already dark, and Pyetchka too had arrived back, flushed, excited, … when … [the senior camp inmate] finally came on again over the loudspeaker. This time he appealed to the former members of the Kartoffelshäler-Kommando [potato-peeling commando], requesting them to resume their old duties in the kitchens, and all other inmates of the camp to stay awake, until the middle of the night, if need be, because they were going to start cooking a strong goulash soup, and it was only at this point that I slumped back on my pillow in relief, only then that something loosened up inside me, and only then did I also think—probably for the first time in all seriousness—of freedom.[48]

Coda

On his return to Budapest, Gyuri encounters a journalist. The boy, still wearing his striped prison jacket, has gotten on a streetcar. But he has no ticket and no money. The conductor is about to throw him off when the journalist intervenes: " 'Give him a ticket!' handing him, or rather thrusting a coin at the conductor." He then turns to Gyuri.

> "Have you come from Germany, son?" "Yes." "From the concentration camps?" "Naturally." "Which one?" "Buchenwald." Yes, he had heard of it, knew it was "one of the pits of the Nazi hell," as he put it. "Where did they carry you off from?" "Budapest." "How long were you there?" "A year in total." "You must have seen a lot of terrible things," he rejoined, but I said nothing … He fell silent … before starting up again: "Did you have to endure many horrors?" to which I replied that it all depended what he considered to be a horror. No doubt, he declared, his expression now somewhat uneasy, I had undergone a lot of deprivation, hunger, and more likely they had beaten me, to which I said: naturally. "Why, my dear boy," he exclaimed, though, now, so it seemed to me, on the verge of losing his patience, "do you keep on saying 'naturally,' and always about things that are not at all natural?" I told him that in a concentration camp, they *were* natural. "Yes, of course, of course," he says, "they were *there*, but …," and broke off, hesitating slightly, "but … I mean, a concentration camp in itself is *unnatural*," finally hitting on the right word as it were. I didn't even bother saying anything to this, as I was beginning slowly to realize that it seems there are some things you just can't argue about with strangers, the ignorant, with those who, in a certain sense, are mere children so to say.[49]

Gyrui, aware that he has reached his stop, gets off the streetcar. The journalist follows him and suggests that the two of them sit down for a minute. Gyuri makes, what seems to him, a futile attempt to convey his experience—that is, "while one is coming to understand everything," he is "already attending to his new business, living, acting, moving, carrying out each new demand at each new stage," and were it not for this "sequencing in time, … it might well be that neither one's brain nor one's heart would cope with it." To which, the journalist replies: "No, it's impossible to imagine it."[50]

With this exchange, Kertész is issuing a warning. Where, at the outset, he expected his readers to be several steps ahead of Gyuri, he is, here, cautioning them, cautioning us, not, on that account, to substitute our prior knowledge for the narrative, unsettled and unsettling though it may be, that he provides.

An Escape Story: Béla Zsolt

Not until 2004 was an English translation of Béla Zsolt's *Nine Suitcases* published. It ends with his escape from the ghetto in Nagyvárad (then in Hungary, now the Rumanian town of Oradea) and doesn't include fragments that describe his train journey from Bergen-Belsen to Switzerland. The memoir had initially appeared in weekly instalments, from May 30, 1946 to February 24, 1947, in *Haladás*, a journal that Zsolt founded and edited. An edition of *Nine Suitcases* in book form was announced for autumn 1947, but it only materialized in 1980. As to the reasons for this delay: it may have been that Zsolt was discouraged by the hostile political and personal reactions to the serial; then for some decades after his death in 1949, his work remained out of favor with the ruling elite—he was an anti-Communist and a Jew. As Imre Kertész knew full well, public discussion of the Holocaust was frowned upon. And Zsolt's is not an easy book to read: there are plenty of horrors, interspersed with moments of grotesque farce, acidic irony, and grim wit.

Born in 1895 in Komáron in northern Hungary, Zsolt served in the Austro-Hungarian army on the Russian front during the First World War. Even before the war was over—he was gravely wounded in 1918—he began making a name for himself as a writer. In 1920 he moved to Budapest and over the next two decades became one of Hungary's most prolific and best known authors. Along with producing ten novels and four plays, he was a frequent contributor to the liberal press. He was a man of the left, but not the far left. He took aim at the conservative establishment that ruled Hungary and at the growing populist movement that championed an unspoiled Magyar race, unspoiled that is by contamination with Jews. He also took aim at the middle classes of Budapest, and, though himself vilified as a Jew, he satirized his co-religionists with gusto. Sophisticated and bohemian, he spent much of his time in fashionable coffee houses in the company of artists and intellectuals, smoking and drinking to excess, damaging his already weakened health.

In what, then, did Zsolt's Judaism consist? He explained: he "never denied" his "Jewishness, not only out of solidarity and tradition, but also out of bloody-mindedness"; he "never wanted to shake it off, like many others, who can't resign themselves to it as long as they live and who become neurotic because they are constantly trying to shed it." So a "godless and profane" Jew—and one who felt a "deep and genuine sympathy for Jesus and for what the gospels reveal about his moral and social objectives." Zsolt considered himself a better Christian than "the church-going females" he "saw grinning at the edge of the pavement" as he was being marched away.[1]

Recall: in 1944, German forces invaded Hungary and, with Hungarian assistance, immediately began to liquidate the country's Jews. In Komáron, it was "poor people, in civies and uniforms," who deported Zsolt's "mother, ... brothers and sisters," and his "younger sister's four-year-old son." In Nagyvárad, it was the same sort of people who herded him and his wife, Agnes, her parents and her daughter by a previous marriage into the ghetto. The parents and daughter were shipped off to Auschwitz and murdered. Zsolt and Agnes managed to get out—by chance, by a "message-in-a-bottle" that found a helpful and courageous recipient.[2] Zsolt's escape amounts to a fluke, a lucky accident, not a recipe for survival.

Missed opportunity (1)

The first sentence of Zsolt's *Nine Suitcases* reads: "Here I am, lying on my mattress in the middle of the synagogue at the foot of the Ark of the Covenant." He has absolutely nothing: everything he had "has become national property." The gendarmes—"with their red faces, their thick cheekbones, their eyes like black buttons, their chins, made to look even more beastly by the tight straps of their helmets"—had looted his apartment and hauled off the nine suitcases that held his and his wife's possessions, "all the necessities and small luxuries ... [they] had collected."[3] Zsolt exploits the conceit of those suitcases—their magnetic or hypnotic power—to account for his predicament, how he ended up in the Nagyvárad ghetto waiting to be deported to Auschwitz.

Almost five years earlier, in August 1939, with thoughts of emigrating to escape the approaching "fascist war," Agnes had packed all of the couple's clothes and objects into nine suitcases. She "had a mania for having more suitcases than necessary," whereas he liked to travel light. So they never traveled together. On August 26, Zsolt left Budapest for Paris, with a minimum of luggage. Two days later, Agnes arrived at the Gare de l'Est. "Mobilisation had already transformed the city and the station was teeming with conscripted soldiers and their alarmed relatives ... It was with difficulty that I found my wife, deathly pale and sobbing. There was nothing out of the ordinary about a weeping woman, and as she clung to me in panic people thought that I too was setting out for the Maginot Line."[4]

What had happened was this. In Budapest, Agnes had taken the suitcases into the compartment. In Salzburg, she was ordered "to send the ... largest ones, which contained our clothes, to the luggage van." She begged and cried, but to no avail. "At the German border station in Kehl, ... she went to look for the suitcases. They were nowhere to be found. The railwayman informed her that they had been left in Munich as the van was being reloaded ... If only to give her something to hope for, he asked for her Paris address and promised to send the suitcases on after her, cash on delivery, if the war hadn't started by the time the next train arrived, and if they were on it."[5]

The following day, after a good deal of weeping and wailing on Agnes's part—"I want my red coat! And shoes! And the boxes! ... Everything was in the boxes!"—Zsolt went with her to the Gare de l'Est and called on the station master.

> Within five minutes I could tell that the French would lose the war. In a strong foreign accent I related the suitcase tragedy to the fellow, who responded with understanding and even sympathy. He immediately allowed us to examine the luggage stores in the basement. If by any chance I had been a fascist agent I could have committed the decade's greatest act of sabotage ... [just days] before the outbreak of the war: nothing would have been simpler than setting fire to the Gare de l'Est with one match and thereby dealing an immeasurable blow to French mobilization.

In the afternoon, in hopes of persuading her to "agree to some reasonable solution," Zsolt took Agnes once more to the station. The station master, his face shining with enthusiasm, shouted: "'Madame ... Congratulations! The bridge may have been blown up by now, but your suitcases arrived!' ... The German railwayman really had loaded the suitcases onto the last train. The French and Germans might have been ready to start bombing each other by evening, but the German railwayman, automatically and with professional honesty, had forwarded the ... 'items.'"[6]

It was a short lived victory. October 1939 found Zsolt sitting with Hungarian friends, nerves on edge, "arguing about politics and wondering what to do next." He could have gone to many different places—Cagnes, Madrid, Lisbon, Marrakesh, even America—had he tried harder. He had the visa and the money. He blamed the nine suitcases for foiling him.

> My wife clung to the nine suitcases tooth and nail, and because there was no room for all nine together on the overcrowded train to the Riviera we didn't go to Cagnes. For the same reason we didn't go to Madrid or Lisbon. In those days it wasn't possible to travel on French trains with luggage. Passengers were sitting on the roofs and hanging from the steps, robbing each other. The railways wouldn't accept any express goods and there was no question of getting anywhere with nine suitcases ... Only one train was prepared to accept the nine suitcases, a train with a sleeping car and a dining car ...: the Simplon Express. It was a good train, a blue train ... The *wagon-lit* attendant, as haughtily as in peacetime, lifted the nine suitcases over the heads of the Parisians who, in a panic after the first air raids, were trying to escape without any luggage. The train crossed Switzerland and Italy according to the peacetime schedule. Only, its destination was Budapest.[7]

A fanciful account. Agnes, deeply upset by the war news, finally snapped at Zsolt: "Look here, I'm neither a journalist nor a politician, and I don't care about your ideas. I'm a middle-class woman from Nagyvárad and that's where my parents and my child are. I've no business to be here now there's a war on. I want to be with them!" Zsolt acquiesced. He hastened to the Swiss embassy to get a transit visa—and thus disguised his own "longing for home with the appearance of ... gallantry." And it was from the Swiss embassy that he "cast off to land in the ... synagogue."[8]

In early June 1944, he, or rather Agnes, caught a final glimpse of the suitcases. From a window in the ghetto, she watched the luggage plundered from the Jews of Nagyvárad being piled high. And she swore, here were their suitcases: she had seen the red labels of the French railroad. Then Hungarian and German soldiers loaded the baggage into freight cars, "on which they painted in large white letters: 'A GIFT FROM THE HUNGARIAN NATION TO THEIR BOMBED-OUT GERMAN BROTHERS.'"[9] A fine example of Nazi euphemism.

Missed opportunity (2)

Zsolt is joined by Friedländer who, sitting on the edge of Zsolt's mattress, tells the story of the red-haired Grosz. The young man, along with Friedländer, had been part of a gravedigging detail. At the end of the day, the gendarme guarding the workers let it be known that were a man to disappear, no one would be the wiser: they had not been counted; there was no register. So Grosz slipped away and set off for the Rumanian border, five kilometers distant. Then he took fright. If he got past the frontier, whom could he turn to? He knew no one, had no addresses, had no money. To forge ahead blindly, he was sure, meant certain death. He suddenly turned around and started running until he managed to catch up with the gravediggers. With a "huge sigh of relief, he released the ... fear and tension that had almost blown him apart."[10]

Zsolt had a similar tale to recount. It took place in the Ukraine. After his return to Budapest in 1939, he had spent the better part of two years "conspiring with friends ..., planning, arguing, blustering and showing off about what would need to be done at the decisive moment" and who would "take what action with a cool head and death-defying courage."[11] Nothing came of it. Once Hungary joined Germany in the war against the Soviet Union in June 1941, Jewish men, roughly 100,000 of them, were conscripted into forced labor units.[12] Special attention was devoted to recruiting "prominent professionals ... and businessmen, well-known Zionists and community leaders, and above all those whom local Christians had denounced as 'objectionable'"—even if, as was true of Zsolt, they were in their forties.[13] In the summer of 1942, Zsolt was called up.

One sequence of events stands out in Zsolt's account—his missed opportunity to become a "pheasant," that is, a prisoner of war, and instead his escaping back to the Hungarian side. His narrative begins with February 18, 1943, with him in the forest of Brańsk (now a town in northeastern Poland), digging graves. He had already heard about the German defeat at Stalingrad earlier in the month. That morning Zsolt and his fellow workers received orders to beat a hasty retreat. They promptly set out. "What am I saying 'set out'?—we ran. There's never been such a happy run—in thirty-five degrees of frost [−35ºC], before us the howling blizzard, above our heads the planes, behind our backs the Russian tanks, whose rattle could clearly be heard. We were running, laughing, partly because what we had never believed would happen—that we'd ever get out of there—had happened, and partly because it was no longer a horror story, a false report, or a reckless Jewish and anti-fascist hope that the Germans were being beaten, that we were being beaten."[14]

Having spent a day and a night freezing in the snow storm, without anything to eat, Zsolt, along with two other men, a barber and a burglar, came upon a convoy of sledges carrying Russian peasants, all from a nearby village. The peasants had figured that if they waited in the forest, there was a good chance that the battle would pass them by. Then, while the Russians continued their advance, they could return to their liberated homes along the forest trails behind the front lines. Zsolt and his two companions climbed onto their sledges and took off.

> I had an unimaginable sense of relief—… we were at last "pheasants." In the evening we would reach the village with the Russians and report to the first Russian officer. I would tell him who I was and ask him, if possible to send a message to Moscow for Béla Belázs, Andor Gábor, and Béla Illés or, maybe my friend Sándor Gergely [Hungarian communist writers in exile in Moscow], with whom I used to hatch plots … in the thirties … I thought that these colleagues would arrange for me to be taken somewhere safe, where I could recover physically and even be of some use to them. I would put in a good word for my splendid comrades, the barber and the burglar.[15]

Zsolt's relief quickly gave way to dread. It turned out that the Russians had stopped their advance and taken up positions three villages further back. The battle beyond that line had only been "a reconnaissance and nuisance carried out by an advance armoured guard. The tanks hadn't been followed by the main units and had pulled back." Now the Germans were "cautiously advancing … along the section of the road that they had recently surrendered. For the time being Golukovka, where these villagers lived, was empty: the Russian soldiers had withdrawn and the Germans hadn't yet arrived." The men of the village wanted to make their way through the forest and join the Russian soldiers. "The women wanted to go home at any price ... Their only concern was their unguarded houses ... Of course the women won. The convoy, with the dejected men and the tense, silent women, departed toward the village."[16]

Once there, the three Hungarians found shelter with a teacher. Before long, someone knocked on the door and shouted: "The Germans are here." Zsolt fully appreciated "what happened when German field gendarmes found straggling soldiers in a Russian house ... The soldiers were shot on the spot and the Russians hanged in front of the house to make others less eager to hide fugitives." The three on them took cover. "Soon we heard the slow and steady rhythm of footsteps typical of a patrol hell-bent on doing its worst, followed by the arrogant, merciless knocking on doors, ... draining the blood from the faces of any decent people huddled ... behind them. Now they were inside the house. An immeasurably long time passed ... A door opened—a German spoke in a rough, insolent, almost jovial voice. Now they were deciding which way to go ... For a few moments they just stood there. Then they left."[17] After a very tense and very long fifteen minutes, the teacher told them that the coast was clear.

What to do next? The burglar ventured out, took a look around, and returned to report: "The village is quite empty. The troops aren't here yet and the gendarmes have gone on to the next village ... If we go right now we'll be able to reach the road without any problems. If we meet someone on the road, ... we tell them ... we've ... been left behind ... They can't hurt us if they see us looking for our company." So like the red-haired Grosz, Zsolt determined to "escape back."

> I'll never forget the moment we stepped out into the moonlight. We looked around us with our hearts beating, as if we were running from slavery and afraid of being stopped before we could reach freedom. Only what we were afraid of was that we might get caught before we could make our plan to return to slavery seem plausible and our desire to return to slavery look sincere.[18]

* * *

Zsolt made it to his unit. Initially he and his companions were able to hitch a ride in a Red Cross vehicle to Novogorod-Seveky. After a night in a German hospital, which included a thorough delousing, they learned that their company might be somewhere in the vicinity of Orlovka, seventy-five kilometers west—a three-day trek. Evening was now falling. The best they could find—it was completely dark by then—was a half-burnt-out barn. What happened after that, Zsolt knew only from hearsay. The typhus that had already been inside him in the German hospital broke loose with full force in the barn.

Zsolt subsequently learned that after several days holed up—and hallucinating—in a peasant's kitchen, he was bundled onto a sledge and taken along by the remnant of a labor-sevice unit that had limped into the village. No one expected him to arrive in Orlovka alive. But he did. As punishment for having fallen behind, his commander wanted to have him tied up. He thought better of it once he realized that Zsolt had typhus. Instead he gave orders that Zsolt be taken to the medical unit's hospital.

> There I was examined by an overbearing, thick-set rude doctor with greying temples … When he heard my name, he cursed violently … But I sensed … that there must be some earlier connection between us. He knew at once who I was and what I had been trying to achieve with all the futile and hopeless scribblings I had published for decades in newspapers and books.…
>
> One evening three weeks later, by which time my weight had shrunk to forty-seven kilos …, I staggered to the WC at the end of the corridor. As I was dragging myself back … the doctor came towards me with quick, angry steps. There were only the two of us in the corridor … He suddenly stopped in front of me, grabbed my hand and said in quiet fury:
>
> "To hell with this bloody world! I'm so sorry for you. I'd love to send you home and I'm going to try, but I don't think these bastards will let me."
>
> He left me standing and walked on … The next day he was roaring again … But he saved my life, Friedländer … I was lucky … That's why I say that things could change for the better, that someone or something could turn up by chance, at any moment. Believe me. Friedländer, I can even imagine surviving this hell.[19]

In the ghetto

Agnes had "yelled" at Zsolt: "What do I care about your ideas, your politics, your literature? I'm a middle-class woman from Nagyvárad. I want to go home to my parents and child!"[20] It was because of them that they had returned to

Hungary in late 1939. In March 1944, after Zsolt had spent fifteen months as a forced laborer followed by four months in the Margit Boulevard political prison, the two of them planned to settle in Nagyvárad for the duration of the war.[21] Agnes was not well: she was recovering, slowly, from major surgery. Within days of their arrival, the Germans occupied Hungary, and, within weeks, the roughly 20,000 Jews of Nagyvárad were fenced into a sealed ghetto, in preparation for being deported to Auschwitz.

On February 13, 1944, Agnes's thirteen-year-old daughter, Éva Heyman, started a diary. She continued writing it until May 30, at which point she gave it for safe-keeping to the family's loyal cook, who, thanks to a "friendly gendarme," had managed a quick visit to the ghetto. Once the war was over, Agnes retrieved the diary and had it published. Éva repeatedly voiced her despair: "I don't want to die. I want to live even if it means that I'll be the only [one] ... I would wait for the end of the war in some cellar, or on the roof, or in some secret cranny. I would even let the cross-eyed gendarme ... kiss me, just as long as they didn't kill me, only that they should let me live."[22]

And there had been a chance for her to escape. Days before the ghetto was set up, the head porter of the Pannonia Hotel had come, with forged documents, to take Zsolt to Budapest. Zsolt suggested that if he refused to leave his ailing wife, they "should at least send the child." Agnes agreed, but his "mother-in-law, her contorted face as red as a beetroot, objected":

> "I'm not going to let her go. In Budapest anything could happen to her. A hotel porter! Who knows, he might even sell her!"
>
> We had lost everything, the gendarmes were already clearing out the apartment ... But what weighed most heavily on my mother-in-law was the vision of her granddaughter ending up on the streets. It was the petty-bourgeois dread of moral ruin that made her shudder.
>
> I tried to persuade her that the girl would come to no harm. I had known the head porter for a long time, he was a gentleman, opposed to the Germans, and a decent man. He would immediately take her to some friendly Christian place.
>
> "No, no, no!"
>
> My wife joined in the argument, desperately, aggressively. They almost came to blows.

"How dare you stop her? Will you take the responsibility if the child dies because of your obsession?"

My mother-in-law buckled. Lowering her voice so that my father-in-law, who was walking up and down in the next room, couldn't hear, she turned toward me:

"Listen. Every night since the Germans arrived we've wanted to take cyanide. But each time either I or my husband stopped to ask: yes, but then what will happen to the child?"

So if the child had gone, the old people would have taken cyanide. There is no doubt that they would have ... But—with a sudden burst of callousness— I asked myself: shouldn't the child be saved? ... This child, with her fairy apple face, her eager curiosity, her ambition, her vanity, her starry eyes full of energy—should she stay with us, die with us, just because if she didn't, the old people would take cyanide?

It was up to my wife to make the decision. She adored her father ... And now she had to decide that her child should go to Budapest with the head porter and her father should die as a result. She couldn't do it, she didn't have the nerve to do it. She collapsed in tears. My mother-in-law had won: the child stayed.[23]

* * *

In her last entry, Éva mentioned that her mother and stepfather were whispering about the family's staying in some kind of typhus hospital in the ghetto. A doctor, whom Zsolt hadn't seen before and who turned out to be in charge of the obstetrics department where Agnes was being sheltered, had approached Zsolt. The first transport was to leave the following day:

"I've been sent by your wife, ... She tells me that you had typhus in the Ukraine."

"Yes. I did," I said. "But does that matter now?"

"In Kolozsvár the deportation was stopped because of typhus," he explained ....

He wanted to fake a typhus epidemic and he needed me. Perhaps chiefly because typhus could be detected in the blood even a year later....

The plan wasn't entirely hopeless, assuming that it was true that in Kolozsvár the deportation had been broken off because of typhus ... I immediately sat down with the ... [doctor] to talk matters over ... [He] had only learnt and read about typhus—I, having had it, knew its smallest actual details, expressions and gestures, all its authentic external signs.[24]

The days passed: the fourth transport left; Zsolt and his wife were scheduled to leave the following day. At the last minute, a reprieve. In a hushed voice, the doctor told Zsolt that he was to be taken to the isolation hospital. Only the typhus suspects and their relatives would be allowed to stay behind. Zsolt asked:

"Is my wife staying with me?'
"Your wife is already getting dressed ... Don't put on your shoes—you'll be carried on a stretcher ... and lean on me, try to totter and stumble. You must now have a high fever." ...
I staggered out of the front door ... At first I only saw the stretcher I was laid on. Then I became aware of the women and children standing in a group on the left—the typhus patients' relations, who didn't have to play at being ill. Twenty minutes later the procession started. We crossed the ghetto, which was completely empty now ... The isolation hospital was at the far end ..., in a large forbidding building standing on its own close to the fence ... As soon as we were deposited ... the doctors injected us with abdominal typhus vaccine—which produces a high fever and typhus symptoms—to make sure that any gendarmes or Germans who might come to inspect us wouldn't discover the deception ... It took us to daybreak to settle down. By that time ... British ... and American [forces] were engaged in an unprecedented battle with the troops of the German Atlantic wall ... It was the dawn of 6 June 1944 [D-Day].[25]

By that time, Éva and her grandparents were already en route to Auschwitz.

* * *

Agnes had been led to believe that her daughter and parents would be among those brought to the isolation hospital. She soon discovered that this was not the case. "After a hair-raising nervous attack, followed by a six-hour faint, she was overcome by speechless ... melancholy ... Then she turned to self-flagellation. For two days she writhed on the bare ... floor ...: her operation wound opened and the doctors had to stitch it up again ... When they left her alone for a few minutes, she tore her artery open at the wrist and in a fit of weeping kept biting her fists until they were bleeding ... She frantically demanded to be taken to the gendarmes, put into a wagon and sent after her family … The horrified doctors held her down and gave her an injection to make her sleep. A few days later she had tired herself out and become resigned. She was put into a nurse's coat and given some work to do."[26]

The gendarmes were, in fact, no longer there. Once they had completed their task of emptying the Nagyvárad ghetto, they had been ordered "to other towns to do some more deporting." The isolation hospital with its seven patients, twenty-two family members, and two doctors was now guarded by the local police. They were not so frightening: though they appreciated that they could treat the Jews however they wished, "they preferred being bribed rather than going in for robbery. This had been an ingrained professional custom with them for decades … It was above all their traditional corruption that made them more humane."[27]

Inside the hospital, the captivity felt "less tight, less suffocating"—a situation that practically invited the prisoners "to make plans for escaping." The policemen walked up and down, round the hospital behind the fence and along the street in front of the fence, "as languidly as they had done their duty in peacetime. They strolled to the corner, where the fence turned at a right angle into the next street, and disappeared for a quarter of an hour, leaving the area unguarded." That is, if the blacksmith who lived across the street and who belonged to the Hungarian version of a national socialist party was not on the alert. In his Arrow Cross uniform, he and a pack of his family and apprentices "kept a beady eye, and passed nasty comments, on everything that happened in the hospital and the street from morning till night. They not only made a fuss when somebody seemed to approach the fence with good intentions, but one or other of the gang started shouting as soon as a passer-by turned into the deserted street."[28]

The blacksmith and his gang ranked as the prisoners "most hated enemies"; a young man on a bicycle—a tailor's apprentice and the most skillful striker on the Navgyvárad football (soccer) team—stood as their "best friend." He "turned up six or seven times a day and threw things—cigarettes, bread, onions, newspapers, sometimes even flowers—over the fence every time he zoomed past, without slowing down, so that the policemen wouldn't notice." Somebody "was always waiting for him to approach on his bicycle, and at the last moment threw out a paper pellet. The footballer, like a galloping cowboy, bent down from his saddle at full speed and picked it up."[29]

All this while, Zsolt was shivering with fever. The artificially induced illness had to be renewed every day—or else, the deception could have been discovered. In his state, he could not imagine escaping; he could hardly drag himself to the WC. Then there was Agnes.

> Psychologically, the reactions caused by the emotional traumas she had suffered during these weeks were of a peculiar kind. They resembled most of all a physical illness involving a crisis—pneumonia or meningitis … During the critical days one either dies of the blows …, or one expectedly finds one's feet and is seized by manic activity … [On the eighth day], she suddenly became herself again, straightened up, and vindictively, recklessly went out into the courtyard to watch for the cyclist. She threw out a paper pellet with the text of a telegram to Budapest.[30]

And, as he had for other desperate prisoners, the footballer forwarded the SOS—"a farewell message-in-a bottle"—on her behalf.[31]

* * *

Early one morning—after about two weeks in the isolation hospital—as Zsolt was tossing and turning with a high fever, a doctor approached him. In a low voice, the doctor told Zsolt to follow him to the doctors' room. Agnes was already there. So too was Lili Szabó, the wife of István Szabó, Zsolt's fellow writer.

> Of all our friends in Budapest, the Szabós were most likely to risk everything to save us … I wasn't even very surprised to see Lili here. I didn't even think it strange that she had managed to get into the ghetto past the fence [and] the policemen … Lili was the kind of person who could get in anywhere she wanted to, without using force or guile. She was trusted by everybody at first sight … She … would be allowed through the gate by the most suspicious guard, not because he thought her a VIP, but because he couldn't imagine that her errand wasn't legitimate.[32]

Lili had come to fetch Zsolt and his wife. She had brought forged documents with her: Zsolt as a waiter at the Pannonia Hotel in Budapest, Agnes as a divorced kitchen maid at the same hotel. With their employer's written permission, the two had been spending four days of paid leave in Nagyvárad. As for getting the pair out of the ghetto, Lili had explained to the police inspector that, though they were Jews, most of their relatives, including Lili herself, were Christians. "And modestly, almost imperceptibly, she had slipped him ten thousand pengős."[33]

Without further ado, Lili laid out the plan. From the clothes left behind in the ghetto, Zsolt and his wife should select outfits that matched their forged documents. Dressed appropriately, they were to leave the ghetto at 9:00 that evening. "That was the time when one of the police guards, who had been letting out … people … for a thousand pengős per head, came on duty."[34] The doctors knew the footballer's address, and Lili would arrange with him to escort the couple once they had existed the ghetto. Lili would be waiting for them on the train platform. Having told them what to do, Lili went back into town.

At the appointed hour, Zsolt and Agnes walked toward the gate. "The policeman gave a small start, then opened up one wing" of it.

> It was as if a stage manager had given the signal; the moment we stepped out of the gate a tremendous downpour began, accompanied by … thunder and lightning.…
>
> "Run," I shouted, grabbing my wife's hand. We ran towards the corner, where we were almost imperceptibly joined by a shadow in a raincoat. It was the footballer, who immediately took the lead and made us follow him at the double across the square and the great marketplace. We ran, flustered and anxious … Soon we were no different from the ordinary pedestrians who were trying to escape from the thunderstorm, puffing and panting and struggling against wind and rain. The people running next to us … never suspected anything, never looked at us, never guessed that we weren't escaping from the thunderstorm, but from the gas … The black raincoat with the footballer in it headed towards a dimly lit door. He pulled the door open and we stumbled into the inn, where an innkeeper in shirtsleeves stood behind the counter … The innkeeper was the footballer's brother-in-law. He didn't ask any questions.

What next? "The footballer went out to get a hansom-cab."

> It seemed an eternity till, a few minutes before ten, the footballer returned with a cab driver … We got into the cab … The footballer whispered into my ear that the driver was a friend of his and we needn't be afraid of him, but we didn't say a word during the whole journey. The downpour had abated and seemed to be turning into a steady rain … We reached the station. In the

semi-dark concourse the peasants were sleeping on their baskets and bags. The platform was almost completely dark—the planes came this way every night if they hadn't got rid of their bombs … In front of the waiting room … [Lili] joined us without a word … We crossed the wet rails to track three, where the long dark Budapest train was standing. The footballer got on to … find us seats in a compartment in which there was nothing untoward … We climbed up the steps and sat down in a … third-class carriage.[35]

The slow night train, with a "single-puny engine, had to drag the bombed-out people, the soldiers on leave and the black marketeers of half the country to the capital." It was a quarter to one the following afternoon when Zsolt and his two companions stepped out of the station. He was back in Budapest, where he had lived for decades; where, now, the ghettoization of the Jews was underway; where, now, he had to hide; and where anyone who recognized him could "club" him down "like a rabid dog."[36]

The Kasztner train

On the night of June 30, 1944, Zsolt and his wife, along with 1,682 other Jews, boarded a train leaving Hungary for what they thought was a neutral country. How the two of them came to be included, he did not say. In the selection of passengers, Rezső Kasztner played a crucial role, and his name came to be affixed to the train. It cost SFR seven million in bribes. One hundred and fifty people bought their places, but the vast majority did not have that kind of money. The rich had to pay for the others. Representatives of all communities, trends, opinions, ages, and origins were included, as well as outstanding intellectuals, scientists, and artists. Kasztner himself was a Zionist. On July 8, the train arrived in a transit and exchange camp for Jews at Bergen-Belsen.[37]

In her report on the Eichmann trial, Hannah Arendt was particularly savage about Kasztner. "In his view … it went without saying that a famous Jew had more right to stay alive than an ordinary one … But if the Jewish … pleaders of 'special cases' were unaware of their involuntary complicity, this … must have been very obvious to those who were engaged in the business of murder. They must have felt, at least, that by being asked to make exceptions, and by occasionally granting them, and thus earning gratitude, they had convinced their opponents of the lawfulness of what they were doing."[38]

Telling rhetoric, but poor history. Kasztner, on behalf of the Budapest Relief and Rescue Committee, took on the difficult and controversial task of negotiating with Eichmann's unit. Surprisingly enough, the SS was willing to confer. Reichsführer-SS Heinrich Himmler, eager to start separate peace talks with the Western Allies behind Hitler's back, assumed, absurdly, that the road to Allied leaders lay through "world Jewry," more specifically through Zionists. And Eichmann would never have let 1,684 Jews go without the express orders of his superiors. As Kasztner saw it, a train leaving for a neutral country would have been a first breach in the policy of total murder. He "hoped that the first train would be followed by a second and a third; once a pattern was established, perhaps an attempt could be made to stop the murder machine altogether."[39]

Arendt was not alone in attacking Kasztner. After the war, he had settled in Israel where he worked with David Ben-Gurion's Mapai government. When a journalist published an inflammatory pamphlet about his collaboration with the SS, the government urged him to sue for libel. He did and lost the case in the Jerusalem District Court. Judge Benyamin Halevy, who was later one of the three judges in the Eichmann trial, told Kasztner that he had "sold his soul to the devil." An appeal was filed. In January 1958, the Supreme Court handed down its verdict, clearing Kasztner of most of the accusations against him. Four of the five judges wrote with "compassion, awe, humility, and incredulity—all of the virtues lacking in Halevy's opinion." For Kasztner, the ruling came several months too late. On the night of March 3, 1957, as he returned home, a young man approached him and asked him if he was Kasztner. "Kasztner answered in the affirmative—and then the stranger shot him three times. Kasztner died of his wounds three days later."[40]

What of Zsolt and his wife? Their ordeal did not end. Of the 1,684 on board Kasztner's train, more than 300 reached Switzerland in August 1944; the rest, roughly 1,370, followed in December. Zsolt and his wife were in the latter group. At the war's end, they returned to Budapest. In 1948, after publishing her daughter's diary, Agnes committed suicide. By then, Zsolt—he had resumed his political and journalistic activities and had come under increasing pressure from the country's new communist rulers—was in failing health. He died the following February.

Conclusion

I noted at the outset that history, meaning the professional study of the past, not memory, has become the instrument for recalling the Holocaust. Do the two stand in opposition to each other? Or are they complementary? Writing history and witnessing it may never be congruent: there will always be a tension between the claims of history—to give an objective account of the past—and those of memory—to capture the discrete and the personal. The voices of diarists and memoirists, by dint of their humanness, provide a way to imagine or reimagine the depth and scope of the subjective terrors; and so they resist the flattening effect of a seamless historical narrative and puncture the complacency of scholarly detachment.[1] Above all, they convey the strangeness, the moral rupture, of the Holocaust.

I also mentioned that to be a convincing "I witness," the autobiographer must become a credible "I," he or she must be believable. Believable but not overbearing. The authors I have focused on are saying: don't look at or analyze me, the narrator, look at what I am describing, listen to what I am saying. They have not allowed the "I" they have created to eclipse the worlds they are portraying. Take Primo Levi, for example. It was *his* recollection, and he had to be there in the text—he was the one who saw and suffered. Yet the very horror of his story required an emotional reserve, a reserve that eschewed all excess—a reserve that bordered on self-effacement.

The Holocaust, Imre Kertész remarked, "brought with it a horrible dread—a dread that it might be forgotten."[2] Levi had a recurrent nightmare: he is at home among friends, recounting the ordeal he has survived. But he cannot help noticing that his audience is not following him and that it soon drifts away. Ruth Kluger asked, repeatedly, with real anguish, will anyone pay attention? Instead, she is urged to erase her memory as if it could be wiped away like chalk on a blackboard. Then there is Victor Klemperer. To "bear witness, precise witness"—that, he claimed, was his "heroism."[3]

To bear witness—to preserve the memory of the horror, to resist its extinction—has been the overarching theme. Because the stories of the dead are lost, Primo Levi wrote, the survivors must "speak in their place, by proxy."[4] What other themes have emerged along the way?

1. "Time … Time helps," so Gyuri told the inquisitive journalist in their postwar conversation. He elaborated: "Were it not for … [the] sequencing in time, and were the entire knowledge to crash in upon a person on the spot, at one fell swoop, it might well be that neither one's brain nor one's heart could cope with it."[5] Klemperer, for his part, might fight a rearguard action against recognizing the trajectory of Nazi anti-Semitism, still he was not forced to face that reality all at once. For Levi, enlightenment came with the greatest suddenness. The Muselmänner, he noted, "are beaten by time, they do not begin to learn German and to untangle the fiendish knot of laws and prohibitions until their body is already breaking down, and nothing can save them from selection or from death by exhaustion."[6] It was Gyuri, not he, who came closest to being crushed.

2. Resourcefulness. Albeit, intermittent at best. Głowiński described his younger self as so deadened, so passive and unreflective that he failed to respond to the news that his mother had made her way to the convent sheltering him. Kluger wrote of her decision to escape the forced march at war's end: "We tend to slither into life-changing situations, driven by this or that circumstance. But anyone who has ever made a real decision knows the difference between pushing ahead and being pushed. Our decision to escape was a real, free decision."[7] Levi struck a similar note in talking with Philip Roth about his last ten days in Auschwitz: "I did … feel like Robinson Crusoe, but with one important difference. Crusoe set to work for his individual survival, whereas I and my two French companions were consciously … willing to work … to save the lives of our sick comrades."[8]

3. Luck. In that same interview, Roth maintained that thinking contributed to Levi's survival, that his survival was rooted in his "professional character: the man of precision, the controller of experiments who seeks the principle of order, confronted with the evil inversion of everything he values." Levi demurred, politely, but firmly: "As for survival, … I insist there was no general

rule, except entering the camp in good health and knowing German. Barring this, luck dominated. I have seen the survival of shrewd people and silly people, the brave and the cowardly, 'thinkers' and madmen. In my case, luck played an essential role on at least two occasions: in leading me to meet the Italian bricklayer and in my getting sick only once, but at the right moment."[9]

All of the authors considered in this study would have agreed: there was no algorithm for survival; and, further, there was no particular virtue in having survived and no particular demerit in having succumbed. There is no place for sentimentality here. There are no grounds for feelgood myth-making.

What will become of these stories? My generation is elderly now. For people my age who were children in the immediate aftermath of the Second World War, knowledge of the Holocaust helped shape our political consciousness and orientation to the world. Not so my grandchildren's generation. Will they take the trouble to retrieve the past, to recover it in its specificity and concreteness?

Notes

Introduction

1 Jorge Semprún, quoted in Tony Judt, *Postwar: A History of Europe since 1945* (New York: Penguin Press, 2005), p. 829.
2 I am not claiming to cover the whole gamut of horrors. I have not touched on the experience of those, like the Soviet Jews, whose testimony is not accessible in English.
3 See Philippe Lejeune, *On Autobiography*, trans. Katherine Leary (Minneapolis: University of Minnesota Press, 1989).
4 Clifford Geertz, *Works and Lives: The Anthropologist as Author* (Stanford, CA: Stanford University Press, 1988), pp. 4, 79.
5 Ruth Kluger, *Still Alive: A Holocaust Girlhood Remembered* (New York: Feminist Press, 2001), pp. 66, 109.

Chapter 1

1 See Amos Elon, "The Jew Who Fought to Stay German," *New York Times Magazine*, March 24, 1996, and John Schmid, "An East German Publishing Coup," *New York Times*, October 7, 1996.
2 Peter Gay, "Inside the Third Reich," *New York Times Book Review*, November 22, 1998. See Daniel Jonah Goldhagen, *Hitler's Willing Executioners: Ordinary Germans and the Holocaust* (New York: Knopf, 1996).
3 Gordon A. Craig, "Destiny in Any Case," *New York Review of Books*, December 3, 1998.
4 Omer Bartov, "The Last German," *New Republic*, December 28, 1998. See also Elon, "The Jew Who Fought to Stay German"; Walter Laqueur, "Three Witnesses: The Legacy of Viktor Klemperer, Willy Cohen, and Richard Koch," *Holocaust and Genocide Studies* 10 (1996): 252–266; Paola Traverso, "Victor Klemperers Deutschlandbild–Ein jüdisches Tagebuch? *Tel Aviver Jahrbuch für Deutsche Geschichte* 26 (1997): 307–344; Henry Ashby Turner, Jr., "Victor Klemperer's Holocaust," *German Studies Review* 22 (1999): 385–395; and Steven E. Aschheim, *Scholem, Arendt, Klemperer: Intimate Chronicles in Turbulent Times* (Bloomington: Indiana University Press, 2001), pp. 70–98.

5 Martin Chalmers, preface to Victor Klemperer, *I Will Bear Witness: A Diary of the Nazi Years 1933–1945*, trans. Martin Chalmers, 2 vols. (New York: Random House, 1998–99), 1: vii. See also Johannes Dirschauer, *Tagebuch gegen den Untergang: Zur Faszination Victor Klemperers* (Giessen: Psychosozial-Verlag, 1997), and Peter Jacobs, *Victor Klemperer: Im Kern ein deutsches Gewächs: Eine Biographie* (Berlin: Aufbau, 2000).

6 See Victor Klemperer, *Curriculum Vitae: Erinnerungen 1881–1918*, ed. Walter Nowojski, 2 vols. (Berlin: Augbau-Verlag, 1996), 1: 599–600. For Klemperer's diaries covering the years of the Weimar Republic, see Victor Klemperer, *Leben sammeln, nicht fragen wozu und warum*, ed. Walter Nowojski with the assistance of Christian Löser, 2 vols. (Berlin: Aufbau-Verlag, 1996).

7 Klemperer, *I Will Bear Witness*, 1, April 10, 1933, p. 12.

8 See Heike Liebsch, "'Ein Tier ist nicht rechtloser und gehetzter': Die Verfolgung der jüdischer Bevölkerung Dresdens 1933 bis 1937," p. 74, and Nora Goldenbogen, "'Man wird keinen von ihnen wiedersehen': Die Vernichtung der Dresdener Juden 1938–1945," p. 109. Both in Hannes Heer, ed., *Im Herzen der Finsternis: Victor Klemperer als Chronist der NS-Zeit* (Berlin: Aufbau-Verlag, 1997).

9 Victor Klemperer, *The Language of the Third: LTI, Lingua Tertii Imperii: A Philologist's Notebook*, trans. Martin Brady (London: Continuum, 2006), pp. ix, 6.

10 Klemperer, *I Will Bear Witness*, 2, June 9, 1942, p. 70, and May 27, 1942, p. 61.

11 See ibid., 1, December 5, 1941, p. 448.

12 Klemperer, *Language of the Third Reich*, p. 9.

13 Klemperer, *I Will Bear Witness*, 1, October 6, 1934, p. 91.

14 See ibid., 1, July 21, 1935, p. 128, and March 6, 1936, p. 154.

15 Ibid., 1, December 12, 1933, p. 43, and April 10, 1933, p. 12.

16 Ibid., 1, June 17, 1934, p. 73.

17 Ibid., 1, September, 16, 1935, p. 131; March 31, 1936, p. 157; and February 11, 1936, p. 153 (emphasis in the original).

18 Ibid., 1, September 29, 1934, p, 89; January 24, 1936, p. 149; April 12, 1936, p. 159; and April 24, 1936, p. 160.

19 Ibid., 1, October 4, 1936, p. 193, and November 26, 1936, p. 200.

20 Ibid., 1, December 6, 1938, p. 279, and June 29, 1938, p. 260.

21 Ibid., 1, May 2, 1935, p. 119; November 9, 1933, p. 40; and December 12, 1933, p. 44 (emphasis in the original).

22 Klemperer, *Language of the Third Reich*, p. 10.

23 Ibid., p. 10.

24 Klemperer, *I Will Bear Witness*, 1, November 25, 1938, p. 274, and November 27, 1938, pp. 275–276.

25 Ibid., 1, November 27, 1938, p. 276; December 3, 1938, p. 278; December 15, 1938, p. 280; and March 6, 1939, p. 295.

26 Ibid., 1, April 14, 1939, p. 381, and July 27, 1941, p. 424.

27 Ibid., 1, July 9, 1933, p. 24; May 2, 1935, p. 120; and June 9, 1941, pp. 388–389 (emphasis in the original).

28 Ibid., 1, July 24, 1940, p. 350; December 20, 1940, p. 365; February 25, 1941, p. 376; and 2, March 24, 1942, p. 32.

29 Ibid, 1, July 9, 1933, p. 23; June 13, 1934, pp. 68–69; and November 12, 1939, p. 319 (emphasis in the original).

30 Ibid., 1, May 15, 1941, p. 385; April 3, 1933, p. 11; July 14, 1934, pp. 74–75; February 2, 1934, p. 53; and October 18, 1936, p. 199.

31 Saul Friedländer, *Nazi Germany and the Jews*, 2 vols. (New York: HarperCollins, 1997–2007), 1: 291.

32 Klemperer, *I Will Bear Witness*, 1, April 5, 1938, p. 253.

33 Ibid., 1, October 9, 1938, p. 272.

34 Ibid., 1, May 26, 1940, pp. 339–341, and 2, September 2, 1942, p. 136 (emphasis in the original).

35 Ibid., 1, May 26, 1940, pp. 340–342; November 18, 1941, p. 444; 2, August 25, 1942, p. 132; and March 6, 1942, p. 24.

36 Ibid., 1, July 6, 1940, pp. 345–346; November 21, 1941, p. 445; and 2, May 22, 1942, p. 55.

37 Ibid., 2, February 15, 1942, p. 15; June 11, 1942, pp. 73–74; and August 20, 1942, pp. 126–127 (emphasis in the original).

38 Ibid., 2, August 25, 1942, p. 132.

39 Ibid., 2, September 1, 1942, p. 136; September 4, 1942, p. 137; and September 28, 1942, pp. 149–150.

40 Ibid., 2, April 16, 1943, p. 213.

41 Ibid., 2, June 24, 1943, p. 328, and May 21, 1943, p. 231.

42 Ibid., 2, October 7, 1943, p. 267, and May 22, 1943, p. 233 (emphasis in the original).

43 Ibid., 2, May 29, 1943, p. 234, and January 14, 1943, p. 391 (emphasis in the original).

44 Ibid., 2, October 1, 1943, p. 266; June 19, 1942, p. 81; March 4, 1943, p. 206; and June 10, 1943, p. 237.

45 Victor Klemperer, *The Lesser Evil: The Diaries of Victor Klemperer 1945–1959*, abridged and trans. Martin Chalmers (London: Weidenfeld and Nicolson, 2003), September 24, 1945, p. 56.

46 Klemperer, *I Will Bear Witness*, 2, June 19, 1942, p. 81; January 24, 1943, p. 192; and October 27, 1942, p. 158.

47 Ibid., 2, December 12, 1943, p. 277, and December 14, 1943, p. 278.

48 Ibid., 2, April 20, 1945, p. 457, and February 21, 1945, p. 420.

49 Ibid., 2, February 22–24, 1945, pp. 407–409.

50 Ibid., 2, February 19, 1945, p. 415, and March 23, 1945, p. 436 (emphasis in the original).

51 Ibid., 2, May 8, 1945, p. 476; May 15, 1945, pp. 479–480; and May 26, 1945, p. 494.

52 Ibid., 2, May 29–June 10, 1945, p. 514.

53 See Steven E. Aschheim, "Comrade Klemperer: Communism, Liberalism, and Jewishness in the DDR. The Later Diaries 1945–59," *Journal of Contemporary History* 36 (2001): 325–343.

54 Klemperer, *The Lesser Evil*, July 26, 1945, p. 30; November 20, 1945, p. 72; and August 12, 1947, p. 212 (emphasis in the original).

Chapter 2

1 Saul Friedländer, *Nazi Germany and the Jews*, 2 vols. (New York: HarperCollins, 1997–2007), 1: 5.

2 Ruth Kluger, *Still Alive: A Holocaust Girlhood Remembered* (New York: Feminist Press, 2001), p. 208. See also Ruth Klüger, *weiter leben: Eine Jugend* (Göttingen: Wallstein, 1992), and *unterwegs verloren: Erinnerungen* (Vienna: Paul Zsolnay, 2008), pp. 155–176. With books in German, Kluger spells her name with an umlaut; in English, she drops the accent. For her further reflections, see Ruth Kluger, "The Future of Holocaust Literature," *German Studies Review* 37 (2014): 391–403. For reviews of *Still Alive*, see Lore Dickstein, "Betrayal Begins at Home," *New York Times*, December 9, 2001; Eunice Lipton, "Survival Skills," *Women's Review of Books* 19.4 (January 2002): 11–12; Gabriele Annan, "Surviving," *New York Review of Books*, November 7, 2002; and Linda Schulte-Sasse, " 'Living on' in the American Press: Ruth Kluger's 'Still Alive' and Its Challenge to a Cherished Holocaust Paradigm," *German Studies Review* 27 (2004): 469–475. For helpful commentary, see Pascale R. Bos, *German-Jewish Literature in the Wake of the Holocaust: Grete Weil, Ruth Klüger, and the Politics of Address* (New York: Palgrave, 2005), pp. 71–88.

3 Kluger, *Still Alive*, pp. 208, 210.

4 Ibid., pp. 68–69, 67 (emphasis in the original).

5 Ibid., pp. 15, 17.

6 Ibid., pp. 20–21 (emphasis in the original).

7 Ibid., p. 28.

8 Ibid., p. 83.

9   Ibid., pp. 35, 36, 39 (emphasis in the original).

10 Ibid., pp. 26, 35, 58, 57 (emphasis in the original).

11 Ibid., pp. 22, 41.

12 Ibid. pp. 55, 58.

13 Ibid., p. 73.

14 Ibid., p. 70.

15 Ibid., pp. 87, 74.

16 Ibid., pp. 86, 75.

17 Ibid., pp. 84, 76, 87 (emphasis in the original).

18 Ibid., p. 86.

19 Ibid., p. 94.

20 Ibid., p. 92.

21 Otto Dov Kulka, *Landscapes of the Metropolis of Death: Reflections on Memory and Imagination*, trans. Ralph Mandel (Cambridge, MA: Harvard University Press, 2013), p. 105. See also Nili Keren, "The Family Camp," in Yisrael Gutman and Michael Berenbaum, eds., *Anatomy of the Auschwitz Death Camp* (Bloomington: Indiana University Press, 1994), pp. 428–440.

22 See Kulka, *Landscapes of the Metropolis of Death*, p. 107.

23 Kluger, *Still Alive*, pp. 103–105 (emphasis in the original).

24 Ibid., pp. 105–108.

25 Ibid., pp. 108, 106.

26 Ibid., pp. 117, 126.

27 Ibid., pp. 118, 117.

28 Ibid., pp. 124, 125.

29 Danial Blatman, *The Death Marches: The Final Phase of the Nazi Genocide*, trans. Chaya Galai (Cambridge, MA: Harvard University Press, 2011), pp. 1, 2. Nikolaus Wachsmann gives a figure of 150,000 dead: see his *kl: A History of the Nazi Concentration Camps* (New York: Farrar, Straus and Giroux, 2015), p. 767n184. Clearly it is impossible to arrive at an exact number.

30 Kluger, *Still Alive*, pp. 122, 137.

31 Ibid., pp. 142, 143.

32 Ibid., p. 149.

33 Ibid., p. 151.

34 Ibid., pp. 176–178.

35 Ibid., p. 184 (emphasis in the original).

36 Michał Głowiński, *The Black Seasons*, trans. Marci Shore (Evanston, IL: Northwestern University Press, 2005), pp. 3, 103.

37 Ibid., p. 5.

38 Ibid., p. 13.

39 Ibid., pp. 6, 7.

40 Ibid., p. 9.

41 Ibid., pp. 10–11.

42 Ibid., p. 12.

43 Ibid., pp. 13–16.

44 Ibid., pp. 42, 33.

45 Ibid., pp. 41, 43.

46 Ibid., p. 60.

47 Ibid., p. 62.

48 Ibid., pp. 63, 65 (emphasis in the original).

49 Ibid., pp. 64, 65.

50 Ibid., p. 77.

51 Ibid., pp. 77–78.

52 Ibid., p. 80.

53 Ibid., p. 81.

54 Ibid., pp. 92, 91.

55 Ibid., pp. 92–95.

56 Ibid., p. 95.

57 Ibid., p. 97.

58 Ibid., pp. 111, 115.

59 Ibid., pp. 116–117.

60 Ibid., pp. 120–123.

61 Ibid., pp. 123, 124.

62 Ibid., pp. 131–132.

63 Ibid., pp.130, 131.

64 Ibid., pp. 164, 125–126.

65 Ibid., pp. 126–127.

66 Ibid., p. 127.

67 Ibid., p. 129.

68 Ibid., pp. 134, 137.

69 Kluger, *Still Alive*, p. 138.

70 Głowiński, *Black Seasons*, p. 59.

Chapter 3

1 Primo Levi, *If This Is a Man*, trans. Stuart Woolf, in *The Complete Works of Primo Levi*, ed. Ann Goldstein, 3 vols. (New York: Liveright, 2015), 1: 57.

2 See Primo Levi, *The Voice of Memory: Interviews 1961–1987*, ed. Marco Belpoliti and Robert Gordon, trans. Robert Gordon (New York: New Press, 2001),

pp. 162, 250. The most useful biography of Levi is Ian Thomson, *Primo Levi* (London: Hutchison, 2002). See also Myriam Anissimov, *Primo Levi: The Tragedy of an Optimist*, trans. Steve Cox (Woodstock, NY: Overlook Press, 1998), and Carole Angier, *The Double Bond: Primo Levi, A Biography* (New York: Farrar, Straus and Giroux, 2002). I have found the following critical appraisals to be helpful: Robert S. C. Gordon, *Primo Levi's Ordinary Virtues: From Testimony to Ethics* (Oxford: Oxford University Press, 2001); Robert S. C. Gordon, ed., *The Cambridge Companion to Primo Levi* (Cambridge: Cambridge University Press, 2007); Jonathan Druker, *Primo Levi and Humanism after Auschwitz: Posthumanist Reflections* (New York: Palgrave Macmillan, 2009); Risa Sodi and Millicent Marcus, eds., *New Reflections on Primo Levi: Before and After Auschwitz* (New York: Palgrave Macmillan, 2011); and Nancy Harrowitz, *Primo Levi and the Identity of a Survivor* (Toronto: University of Toronto Press, 2016).

3 Primo Levi, *The Periodic Table*, trans. Ann Goldstein, in *Complete Works* 2: 782, 785.

4 Ibid., p. 800.

5 Ibid., pp. 858–859.

6 Levi, *If This Is a Man*, p. 9. See Sergio Luzzatto, *Primo Levi's Resistance: Rebels and Collaborators in Occupied Italy*, trans. Frederika Randall (New York: Metropolitan, 2016).

7 Levi, *The Periodic Table*, p. 861.

8 Levi, *The Voice of Memory*, pp. 69, 102.

9 Levi, *If This Is a Man*, p. 82.

10 Ibid., p. 5.

11 Primo Levi, *The Drowned and the Saved*, trans. Michael F. Moore, in *Complete Works* 3: 2466–2467.

12 Levi, *If This Is a Man*, p. 25 (emphasis in the original).

13 Ibid., p. 12 (emphasis in the original).

14 See Primo Levi with Leonardo de Benedetti, *Auschwitz Report*, ed. Robert S. C. Gordon, trans. Judith Woolf (London: Verso, 2006), pp. 32–35.

15 See Primo Levi, *Uncollected Stories and Essays: 1949–1980*, trans. Alessandra Bastagli and Francesco Bastagli, in *Complete Works* 2: 1298.

16 Levi, *If This Is a Man*, pp. 15–16.

17 Nikolaus Wachsmann, *kl: A History of the Nazi Concentration Camps* (New York: Farrar, Straus and Giroux, 2015), pp. 345, 453.

18 Levi, *If This Is a Man*, pp. 18, 19, 23, 22 (emphasis in the original).

19 Ibid., p. 24 (emphasis in the original).

20 Ibid., pp. 29–30 (emphasis in the original).

21 Ibid., p. 30 (emphasis in the original).

22 Ibid., pp. 30, 31 (emphasis in the original).

23 Ibid., pp. 56, 58, 59.

24 Ibid., pp. 32–33.

25 Ibid., pp. 83, 85 (emphasis in the original). To improve his chances of survival, Levi took German lessons from a fellow prisoner, paying him with bread: see Levi, *The Drowned and the Saved*, pp. 2474–2475, 2478–2479.

26 Levi, *If This Is a Man*, pp. 39, 40.

27 Ibid., p. 85.

28 Ibid., pp. 85–87 (emphasis in the original).

29 See Angier, *The Double Bond*, p. 346.

30 Levi, *If This Is a Man*, p. 88.

31 Ibid., p. 89.

32 Ibid., pp. 89–90 (emphasis in the original).

33 Ibid., p. 115.

34 Primo Levi, *Lilith and Other Stories*, trans. Ann Goldstein, in *Complete Works* 2: 1403.

35 Ibid., pp. 1404, 1403.

36 Ibid., p. 1357.

37 Levi, *If This Is a Man*, p. 113.

38 Ibid., p. 116.

39 Ibid., pp. 100–101 (emphasis in the original).

40 Ibid., p. 131.

41 Ibid., p. 119 (emphasis in the original).

42 Ibid., pp. 120, 122.

43 Ibid., pp. 122, 123.

44 Ibid., pp. 123–124.

45 Ibid., pp. 133, 132 (emphasis in the original).

46 Ibid., pp. 133, 135.

47 Ibid., p. 134.

48 Ibid., p. 136.

49 Ibid., p. 134.

50 Primo Levi, *Stories and Essays*, trans. Anne Milano Appel, in *Complete Works* 3: 2292.

51 Ibid., pp. 2291–2293.

52 Levi, *If This Is a Man*, p. 132.

53 See Daniel Blatman, *The Death Marches: The Final Phase of Nazi Genocide*, trans. Chaya Galai (Cambridge, MA: Harvard University Press, 2011), p. 81.

54 See Wachsmann, *kl*, pp. 558–560. See also Blatman, *The Death Marches*, pp. 79–97, and Marc Masurovsky, "Visualizing the Evacuations from the Auschwitz-Birkenau Camp System: When Does an Evacuation Turn into a Death

March?" in Jean-Luc Blondel, Susanne Urban, and Sebastian Schönemann, eds., *Freilungen: Auf den Spuren der Todesmärsche* (Göttingen: Wallstein, 2012), pp. 108–121.

55 Levi, *If This Is a Man*, p. 148.

56 Ibid., p. 149.

57 H. Stuart Hughes, *Prisoners of Hope: The Silver Age of the Italian Jews 1924–1974* (Cambridge, MA: Harvard University Press, 1983), p. 78.

58 Levi, *If This Is a Man*, p. 149.

59 Ibid., pp. 151, 152.

60 Ibid., p. 155.

61 Ibid., pp. 154, 157.

62 Ibid., pp. 153, 157, 158.

63 Ibid., pp. 158–159, 164.

64 Primo Levi, *The Truce*, trans. Ann Goldstein, in *Complete Works* 1: 216.

65 Levi, *If This Is a Man*, pp. 93–95 (emphasis in the original).

66 Paul Steinberg, *Speak You Also: A Survivor's Reckoning*, trans. Linda Coverdale (New York: Picador, 2000), p. 138. For commentary, see Susanna Egan, "The Drowned and the Saved: Primo Levi and Paul Steinberg in Dialogue," *History and Memory* 13 (2001): 96–112.

67 Steinberg, *Speak You Also*, pp. 48, 63 (emphasis in the original).

68 Ibid., p. 39.

69 Ibid., pp. 34–35, 37, 38, 39–40.

70 Ibid., p. 8.

71 Ibid., pp. 5, 7–8.

72 Ibid., pp. 100–101.

73 Angier, *The Double Bond*, p. 781.

74 See Steinberg, *Speak You Also*, p. 47.

75 Ibid., pp. 54, 46, 71, 70.

76 Ibid., pp. 75, 76, 87.

77 Levi, *If This Is a Man*, p. 94.

78 Steinberg, *Speak You Also*, pp. 88–89.

79 Ibid., pp. 121, 125–126.

80 Ibid., p. 126.

81 Ibid., pp.130–131.

82 See Susan Tarrow, "Remembering Primo Levi: A Conversation with 'Il Pikolo del Kommando 98,'" *Forum Italicum: Journal of Italian Studies* 28 (1994): 101–110.

83 Levi, *If This Is a Man*, pp. 106–109 (emphasis in the original).

84 Ibid., p. 109.

Chapter 4

1 For the events in Hungary, see Randolph L. Braham, *The Politics of Genocide: The Holocaust in Hungary*, 3rd ed., 2 vols. (New York: Columbia University Press, 2016). See also Christian Gerlach and Götz Aly, *Das letzte Kapitel: Realpolitik, Ideologie und der Mord an den ungarischen Juden 1944–1945* (Stuttgart: Deutsche Verlags-Anstalt, 2002).

2 Rafi Benshalom, *We Struggled for Life: The Hungarian Zionist Youth Resistance during the Nazi Era* (Jerusalem: Gefen, 2001), pp. 8–10, quoted in Zoltán Vági, László Csősz, and Gábor Kádár, eds., *The Holocaust in Hungary: Evolution of a Genocide* (Lanham, MD: AltaMira Press, 2013), p. xlvii.

3 See Randolph L. Braham, "Hungarian Jews," in Yisrael Gutman and Michael Berenbaum, eds. *Anatomy of the Auschwitz Death Camp* (Bloomington: Indiana University Press, 1994), p. 465.

4 Imre Kertész, *The Holocaust as Culture*, trans. Thomas Cooper (London: Seagull Books, 2011), pp. 40–41. Kertész did celebrate a bar mitzvah at age thirteen: see Imre Kertész, *Dossier K*, trans. Tim Wilkinson (Brooklyn, NY: Melville House, 2013), pp. 42–43.

5 Imre Kertész, "Nobel Lecture 2002: Heureka," www.nobelprize.org/nobel_prizes/literature/laureates/2002/kertész-lecture-e.html, pp. 3–4.

6 Kertész, *Dossier K*, p. 8. For useful commentary on *Fatelessness*, see István Déak, "Stranger in Hell," *New York Review of Books*, September 25, 2003; Louise O. Vasvári and Steven Tötösy de Zepetnek, eds., *Imre Kertész and Holocaust Literature* (West Lafayette, IN: Purdue University Press, 2005); Margrit Frölich, "Jenseits der Tatsachen und Erinnerungen: Imre Kertész' *Roman eines Schicksallosen* als literarisches Zeugnis des Holocaust," in Michael Elm and Gottfried Kössler, eds., *Zeugenschaft des Holocaust: Zwischen Trauma, Tradierung und Ermittlung* (Frankfurt: Campus Verlag, 2007), pp. 230–245; J. Hillis Miller, *The Conflagration of Community: Fiction before and after Auschwitz* (Chicago: University of Chicago Press, 2011), pp. 177–227; and Susan Derwin, *Rage Is the Subtext: Readings in Holocaust Literature and Film* (Columbus: Ohio State University Press, 2012), pp. 79–105.

7 Imre Kertész, *Fatelessness*, trans. Tim Wilkinson (New York: Vintage, 2004), p. 3.

8 Kertész wrote the screenplay for a movie version, made in Hungary and entitled *Fateless*, that was released in 2005. Using very short scenes that fade to black, it captures the main events of the book; but it does not reproduce the ironic tone.

9 Kertész, "Nobel Lecture," p. 4.

10 The lack of distinction between present and past has prompted me to refer to the narrator/protagonist by his first name.

11 Kertész, *Fatelessness*, pp. 260, 258, 261, 259.

12 Primo Levi, *If This Is a Man*, trans. Stuart Woolf, in *The Complete Works of Primo Levi*, ed. Ann Goldstein, 3 vols. (New York: Liveright, 2015), 1: 85.

13 Primo Levi, *The Drowned and the Saved*, trans. Michael F. Moore, in *Complete Works* 3: 2468–2469.

14 For a discussion of witnessing and the Muselmann, see Giogio Agamben, *Remnants of Auschwitz: The Witness and the Archive*, trans. Daniel Heller-Roazen (New York: Zone Books, 1999), pp. 41–86.

15 Kertész, *Fatelessness*, p. 28.

16 Ibid., pp. 40–41.

17 Ibid., pp. 52–56.

18 Ibid., pp. 56, 57.

19 Ibid., p. 249.

20 Ibid., pp. 59, 63.

21 Ibid., pp. 63–64.

22 Ibid., pp. 76–79 (emphasis in the original).

23 Ibid., pp. 82, 85–86 (emphasis in the original).

24 Ibid., pp. 110–112.

25 Ibid., p. 113 (emphasis in the original).

26 Ibid., p. 124 (emphasis in the original).

27 Ibid., p. 128.

28 See Nikolaus Wachsmann, *kl: A History of the Nazi Concentration Camps* (New York: Farrar, Straus and Giroux, 2015), pp. 465–466.

29 Kertész, *Fatelessness*, 135–136.

30 Kertész, *Dossier K*, pp. 12–13.

31 Kertész, *Fatelessness*, pp. 132, 136–137.

32 Ibid., pp. 145, 144, 147.

33 Ibid., pp. 149, 165, 171–173 (emphasis in the original).

34 Ibid., p. 173.

35 Ibid., pp. 181–182, 180, 183.

36 Ibid., pp. 184, 185, 186–187 (emphasis in the original).

37 Ibid., pp. 187, 189. In his Nobel lecture, Kertész told his audience that while he was preparing his address he received a package from the director of the Buchenwald Memorial Center. It contained a copy of the daily report for February 18, 1945. In the "Decrement" column, Kertész saw listed Prisoner #64921, Imre Kertész, factory worker, born 1927. Two of the data were false: Kertész had made himself two years older than he was and had claimed to be a worker, not a student. Both lies aimed, successfully, at making him seem more useful to his captors. Kertész, "Nobel Lecture 2002: Heureka," p. 6.

38 Kertész, *Fatelessness*, pp. 200, 201 (emphasis in the original).

39 Ibid., pp. 207, 225.

40 Ibid., p. 208.

41 Ibid., pp. 229, 226 (emphasis in the original).

42 See Daniel Blatman, *The Death Marches: The Final Phase of Nazi Genocide*, trans. Chaya Galai (Cambridge, MA: Harvard University Press, 2011), p. 97.

43 Kertész, *Fatelessness*, p. 229 (emphasis in the original).

44 Ibid., p. 230.

45 See Blatman, *Death Marches*, p. 151, and Wachsmann, *kl*, p. 579.

46 Kertész, *Fatelessness*, pp. 233, 234 (emphasis in the original).

47 Eugen Kogon, *The Theory and Practice of Hell: German Concentration Camps and the System Behind Them*, trans. Heinz Norden (New York: Farrar, Straus, 1950), p. 257.

48 Kertész, *Fatelessness*, pp. 235, 234, 236 (emphasis in the original).

49 Ibid., pp. 246–248 (emphasis in the original).

50 Ibid., pp. 249, 250.

Chapter 5

1   Béla Zsolt, *Nine Suitcases: A Memoir*, trans. Ladislaus Löb (New York: Schocken Books, 2004), p. 119.

2   Ibid., pp. 275, 255.

3   Ibid., pp. 1, 9.

4   Ibid., p. 33.

5   Ibid., p. 34.

6   Ibid., pp. 34, 36, 37.

7   Ibid., pp. 15–17 (emphasis in the original).

8   Ibid., pp. 17–18.

9   Ibid., p. 260 (capital letters in the original).

10 Ibid., p. 71.

11 Ibid., p. 21.

12 See Robert Rozett, *Conscripted Slaves: Hungarian Jewish Forced Laborers on the Eastern Front during the Second World War* (Jerusalem: Yad Vashem, 2013), p. 60.

13 Randolph L. Braham, *The Hungarian Labor Service System, 1939–1945* (New York: Columbia University Press, 1977), p. 27

14 Zsolt, *Nine Suitcases*, p. 135.

15 Ibid., pp. 154–155.

16 Ibid., p. 157.

17 Ibid., pp. 158, 159.

18 Ibid., p. 160.

19 Ibid., pp. 188–192.

20 Ibid., pp. 236–237.

21 Zsolt wrote that he "spent nineteen months as a forced labourer in Russia," ibid.,
    p. 216. His stepdaughter refers to fifteen months, which given the chronology
    seems more plausible. Adding the four months he was jailed as a political
    prisoner, one gets to a total of nineteen. See Éva Heyman, *The Diary of Éva
    Heyman*, trans. Misha M. Kohn (New York: Shapolsky, 1988), p. 43.

22 Heyman, *Diary*, p. 104.

23 Zsolt, *Nine Suitcases*, pp. 231–233.

24 Ibid., pp. 125–129.

25 Ibid., pp. 244–245.

26 Ibid., pp. 248–249.

27 Ibid., pp. 246–248.

28 Ibid., pp. 248, 252.

29 Ibid., pp. 251–252, 255.

30 Ibid., p. 257.

31 Ibid., p. 255.

32 Ibid., p. 263.

33 Ibid., p. 264.

34 Ibid., p. 264.

35 Ibid., pp. 267–270.

36 Ibid., pp. 272, 321.

37 Two recent books on the Kasztner train are Anna Porter, *The Kasztner Train: The
    True Story of an Unknown Hero of the Holocaust* (New York: Walker, 2007), and
    Ronald Florence, *Emissary of the Doomed: Bargaining for Lives in the Holocaust*
    (New York: Viking, 2010). The most reliable and scholarly account remains
    Yehuda Bauer, *Jews for Sale? Nazi-Jewish Negotiations, 1933–1945* (New Haven,
    CT: Yale University Press, 1994).

38 Hannah Arendt, *Eichmann in Jerusalem: A Report on the Banality of Evil*, rev.
    and enlarged ed. (New York: Penguin, 2006), pp. 132–133.

39 Bauer, *Jews for Sale?* p. 198.

40 Tom Segev, *The Seventh Million: The Israelis and the Holocaust*, trans. Haim
    Watzman (New York: Hill and Wang, 1993), pp. 306, 308.

Conclusion

1 See Saul Friedländer, *Nazi Germany and the Jews*, 2 vols.
   (New York: HarperCollins, 1997–2007), 2: xxvi, and his *Memory, History and*

the *Extermination of the Jews of Europe* (Bloomington: Indiana University Press, 1993), pp. 85–101.

2   Imre Kertész, *The Holocaust as Culture*, trans. Thomas Cooper (London: Seagull Books, 2011), p. 59.

3   Victor Klemperer, *I Will Bear Witness: A Diary of the Nazi Years 1933–1945*, trans. Martin Chalmers, 2 vols. (New York: Random House, 1998–99), 2, May 27, 1942, p. 61.

4   Primo Levi, *The Drowned and the Saved*, trans. Michael F. Moore, in *The Complete Works of Primo Levi*, ed. Ann Goldstein, 3 vols. (New York: Liveright, 2015), 3: 2469.

5   Imre Kertész, *Fatelessness*, trans. Tim Wilkerson (New York: Vintage, 2004), p. 249.

6   Primo Levi, *If This Is a Man*, trans. Stuart Woolf, in *Complete Works* 1: 85.

7   Ruth Kluger, *Still Alive: A Holocaust Girlhood Remembered* (New York: Feminist Press, 2001), p. 130.

8   "A Conversation with Primo Levi by Philip Roth," in Primo Levi, *Survival in Auschwitz: The Nazi Assault on Humanity*, trans. Stuart Woolf (New York: Simon and Schuster, 1996), p. 180.

9   Ibid., p. 180.

Select Bibliography

Adler, H. G. *Theresienstadt 1941-1945: The Face of a Coerced Community*. Translated by Belinda Cooper. Cambridge: Cambridge University Press, 2017.

Agamben, Giogio. *Remnants of Auschwitz: The Witness and the Archive*. Translated by Daniel Heller-Roazen. New York: Zone Books, 1999.

Allen, Michael Thad. *The Business of Genocide: The SS, Slave Labor, and the Concentration Camps*. Chapel Hill: University of North Carolina Press, 2002.

Aly, Götz. *"Final Solution": Nazi Population Policy and the Murder of the European Jews*. Translated by Belinda Cooper and Allison Brown. New York: Oxford University Press, 1999.

Améry, Jean. *At the Mind's Limits: Contemplations by a Survivor on Auschwitz and Its Realities*. Translated by Sidney Rosenfeld and Stella P. Rosenfeld. Bloomington: Indiana University Press, 1980.

Angier, Carole. *The Double Bond: Primo Levi, A Biography*. New York: Farrar, Straus and Giroux, 2002.

Anissimov, Myriam. *Primo Levi: The Tragedy of an Optimist*. Translated by Steve Cox. Woodstock, NY: Overlook Press, 1998.

Annan, Gabriele. "Surviving." *New York Review of Books*, November 7, 2002.

Appelfeld, Aharon. "Individualization of the Holocaust." In *Holocaust Chronicles: Individualizing the Holocaust through Diaries and Other Contemporaneous Personal Accounts*. Edited by Robert Moses Shapiro. Hoboken, NJ: Ktav, 1999.

Arendt, Hannah. *The Origins of Totalitarianism*. New York: Harcourt, Brace, 1951.

Arendt, Hannah. *Eichmann in Jerusalem: A Report on the Banality of Evil*. Revised and enlarged ed. New York: Penguin, 2006.

Aschheim, Steven E. *Brothers and Strangers: The East European Jews in German and German Jewish Consciousness, 1800–1923*. Madison: University of Wisconsin Press, 1982.

Aschheim, Steven E. *Culture and Catastrophe: German and Jewish Confrontations with National Socialism and Other Crises*. New York: Macmillan, 1996.

Aschheim, Steven E. "Comrade Klemperer: Communism, Liberalism, and Jewishness in the DDR. The Later Diaries 1945–59." *Journal of Contemporary History* 36 (2001): 325–343.

Aschheim, Steven E. *Scholem, Arendt, Klemperer: Intimate Chronicles in Turbulent Times*. Bloomington: Indiana University Press, 2001.

Balakian, Peter. "Poetry in Hell: Primo Levi and Dante at Auschwitz." *American Poetry Review* 37 (2008): 3–5.

Bankier, David. *The Germans and the Final Solution: Public Opinion under Nazism*. Cambridge, MA: Basil Blackwell, 1992.

Bartov, Omer. *Murder in Our Midst: The Holocaust, Industrial Killing and Representation*. New York: Oxford University Press, 1996.

Bartov, Omer. "The Last German." *New Republic*, December 28, 1998.

Bauer, Yehuda. "The Death Marches, January–May 1945." *Modern Judaism* 3 (1983): 1–21.

Bauer, Yehuda. *Jews for Sale? Nazi-Jewish Negotiations, 1933–1945*. New Haven, CT: Yale University Press, 1994.

Bauer, Yehuda. *Rethinking the Holocaust*. New Haven, CT: Yale University Press, 2001.

Bauman, Zygmunt. *Modernity and the Holocaust*. Ithaca, NY: Cornell University Press, 1989.

Becker, Jurek. *Jakob the Liar*. Translated by Leila Vennewitz. New York: Harcourt Brace Jovanovich, 1975. Reprint. New York: Plume, 1990.

Berg, Mary. *Warsaw Ghetto: A Diary*. Edited by S. L. Shneiderman. Translated by Norbert Guterman and Sylvia Glass. New York: Fischer, 1945.

Bernard-Donals, Michael, and Richard Glejzer. *Between Witness and Testimony: The Holocaust and the Limits of Representation*. Albany: State University of New York Press, 2001.

Bernstein, Michael André. *Foregone Conclusions: Against Apocalyptic History*. Berkeley: University of California Press, 1994.

Bernstein, Michael André. "The 'Schindler's List' Effect." *American Scholar* 63 (1994): 429–432.

Bettelheim, Bruno. "Individual and Mass Behavior in Extreme Situations." *Journal of Abnormal Social Psychology* 38 (1943): 417–452.

Bikont, Anna. *The Crime and the Silence: Confronting the Massacre of Jews in Wartime Jedwabne*. Translated by Alissa Valles. New York: Farrar, Straus and Giroux, 2015.

Blatman, Daniel. *The Death Marches: The Final Phase of the Nazi Genocide*. Translated by Chaya Galai. Cambridge, MA: Harvard University Press, 2011.

Bloxham, Donald. *Genocide on Trial: War Crimes Trials and the Formation of Holocaust History and Memory*. Oxford: Oxford University Press, 2001.

Borowski, Tadeuz. *This Way to the Gas, Ladies and Gentlemen*. Selected and translated by Barbara Vedder. Harmondsworth, UK: Penguin, 1967.

Bos, Pascale R. *German-Jewish Literature in the Wake of the Holocaust: Grete Weil, Ruth Klüger, and the Politics of Address*. New York: Palgrave, 2005.

Braham, Randolph L. *The Hungarian Labor Service System, 1939–1945*. New York: Columbia University Press, 1977.

Braham, Randolph L. *The Politics of Genocide: The Holocaust in Hungary*. 3rd ed., 2 vols. New York: Columbia University Press, 2016.

Brenner, Rachel Feldhay. *Writing as Resistance: Four Women Confronting the Holocaust*. University Park: Pennsylvania State University Press, 1997.

Breznitz, Shlomo. *Memory Fields*. New York: Knopf, 1993.

Brostoff, Anita, ed. *Flares of Memory: Stories of Childhood during the Holocaust*. Oxford: Oxford University Press, 2001.

Browning, Christopher R. *Nazi Policy, Jewish Workers, German Killers*. New York: Cambridge University Press, 2000.

Browning, Christopher R. *Collected Memories: Holocaust History and Postwar Testimony*. Madison: University of Wisconsin Press, 2003.

Browning, Christopher R. *Remembering Survival: Inside a Nazi Slave-Labor Camp*. New York: Norton, 2010.

Bruner, Jerome. "The Autobiographical Process." *Current Sociology* (1995): 161–177.

Burleigh, Michael, and Wolfgang Wippermann. *The Racial State: Germany 1933–1945*. New York: Cambridge University Press, 1991.

Caruth, Cathy, ed. *Trauma: Explorations in Memory*. Baltimore, MD: Johns Hopkins University Press, 1995.

Celan, Paul. "Speech on the Occasion of Receiving the Literature Prize of the Free Hanseatic City of Bremen." In *Selected Poems and Prose of Paul Celan*. Translated by John Felstiner. New York: Norton, 2001.

Cesarani, David. *Becoming Eichmann*. New York: DaCapo, 2004.

Cesarani, David. *Final Solution: The Fate of the Jews 1933–1949*. London: Macmillan, 2016.

Chalmers, Martin. Preface to *I Will Bear Witness: A Diary of the Nazi Years 1933–1945*, by Victor Klemperer. Translated by Martin Chalmers. 2 vols. New York: Random House, 1998–99.

Clendinnen, Inga. *Reading the Holocaust*. New York: Cambridge University Press, 1999.

Confino, Alon. "Narrative Form and Historical Sensation: On Saul Friedländer's 'The Years of Extermination.'" *History and Theory* 48 (2009): 199–219.

Confino, Alon. *A World Without Jews: The Nazi Imagination from Persecution to Genocide*. New Haven, CT: Yale University Press, 2014.

Craig, Gordon A. "Destiny in Any Case." *New York Review of Books*, December 3, 1998.

Czerniaków, Adam. *The Warsaw Diary of Adam Czerniakow: Prelude to Doom.* Edited by Raul Hilberg, Stanislaw Staron, and Josef Kermisz. Translated by Stanislaw Staron. New York: Stein and Day, 1979.

Dawidowicz, Lucy. *The War against the Jews 1933–1945.* New York: Holt, Rinehart and Winston, 1975.

Deák, István. "Holocaust Views: The Goldhagen Controversy in Retrospect." *Central European History* 30 (1997): 295–307.

Deák, István. *Essays on Hitler's Europe.* Lincoln: University of Nebraska Press, 2001.

Deák, István. "Stranger in Hell." *New York Review of Books,* September 25, 2003.

Dean, Martin. *Robbing the Jews: The Confiscation of Jewish Property in the Holocaust, 1933–1945.* New York: Cambridge University Press, 2008.

Delbo, Charlotte. *Auschwitz and After.* Translated by Rosette C. Lamont. New Haven, CT: Yale University Press, 1995.

Derwin, Susan. *Rage Is the Subtext: Readings in Holocaust Literature and Film.* Columbus: Ohio State University Press, 2012.

Des Pres, Terrence. *The Survivor: An Anatomy of Life in the Death Camps.* New York: Oxford University Press, 1975.

Dickstein, Lore. "Betrayal Begins at Home." *New York Times,* December 9, 2001.

Dirschauer, Johannes. *Tagebuch gegen den Untergang: Zur Faszination Victor Klemperers.* Giessen: Psychosozial-Verlag, 1997.

Druker, Jonathan. *Primo Levi and Humanism after Auschwitz: Posthumanist Reflections.* New York: Palgrave Macmillan, 2009.

Dwork, Deborah. *Children with a Star: Jewish Youth in Nazi Europe.* New Haven, CT: Yale University Press, 1991.

Egan, Susanna. "The Drowned and the Saved: Primo Levi and Paul Steinberg in Dialogue." *History and Memory* 13 (2001): 96–112.

Ehrenburg, Ilya, and Vasily Grossman. *The Complete Black Book of Russian Jewry.* Edited and translated by David Patterson. New Brunswick, NJ: Transaction, 2002.

Eley, Geoff, ed. *The "Goldhagen Effect": History, Memory, Nazism–Facing the German Past.* Ann Arbor, MI: University of Michigan Press, 2000.

Elon, Amos. "The Jew Who Fought to Stay German." *New York Times Magazine,* March 24, 1996.

Engelking, Barbara, and Jacek Leociak. *The Warsaw Ghetto: A Guide to the Perished City.* New Haven, CT: Yale University Press, 2009.

Ericksen, Robert P. *Complicity in the Holocaust: Churches and Universities in Nazi Germany.* New York: Cambridge University Press, 2012.

Evans, Richard J. *The Third Reich at War: How the Nazis Led Germany from Conquest to Disaster.* London: Allen Lane, 2008.

Ezrahi, Sidra Dekoven. "Representing Auschwitz." *History and Memory* 7 (1995): 122–154.

Felman, Shoshana, and Dori Laub. *Testimony: Crises of Witnessing in Literature, Psychoanalysis, and History*. London: Routledge, 1992.

Felstiner, Mary Lowenthal. *To Paint Her Life: Charlotte Salomon in the Nazi Era*. New York: HarperCollins, 1994.

Figes, Eva. *Tales of Innocence and Experience: An Exploration*. London: Bloomsbury, 2003.

Filip, Müller. *Eyewitness Auschwitz: Three Years in the Gas Chambers*. Edited and translated by Susanne Flatauer. Chicago: Ivan R. Dee, 1999.

Fink, Ida. *A Scrap of Time and Other Stories*. Translated by Madeline Levine and Francine Prose. New York: Pantheon, 1987.

Finkelstein, Norman G. *The Holocaust Industry: Reflections on the Exploitation of Jewish Suffering*. London: Verso, 2000.

Florence, Ronald. *Emissary of the Doomed: Bargaining for Lives in the Holocaust*. New York: Viking, 2010.

Frank, Anne. *The Diary of a Young Girl*. Critical ed. Edited by David Barnouw and Gerrold van Stroom. Translated by Arnold J. Pomerans and B. M. Mooyaart-Doubleday. London: Viking, 1989.

Frankl, Victor E. *Man's Search for Meaning: An Introduction to Logotherapy*. Translated by Ilse Lasch. Boston: Beacon Press, 1959.

Franklin, Ruth. *A Thousand Darknesses: Lies and Truth in Holocaust Fiction*. New York: Oxford University Press, 2011.

Fremont, Helen. *After Long Silence: A Memoir*. New York: Delacorte Press, 1999.

Friedländer, Saul. *L'Antisemitisme: Histoire d'une psychose collective*. Paris: Seuil, 1971.

Friedländer, Saul. *History and Psychoanalysis: An Inquiry into the Possibilities and Limits of Psychohistory*. Translated by Susan Suleiman. New York: Holmes and Mcier, 1978.

Friedländer, Saul. *When Memory Comes*. Translated by Helen R. Lane. New York: Farrar, Straus and Giroux, 1979.

Friedländer, Saul. *Memory, History, and the Extermination of the Jews of Europe*. Bloomington: Indiana University Press, 1993.

Friedländer, Saul. *Nazi Germany and the Jews*. 2 vols. New York: HarperCollins, 1997–2007.

Friedländer, Saul. *Where Memory Leads: My Life*. New York: Other Press, 2016.

Friedländer, Saul, ed. *Probing the Limits of Representation: Nazism and the "Final Solution."* Cambridge, MA: Harvard University Press, 1992.

Fritzsche, Peter. *Life and Death in the Third Reich*. Cambridge, MA: Harvard University Press, 2008.

Frölich, Margrit. "Jenseits der Tatsachen und Erinnerungen: Imre Kertész' *Roman eines Schicksallosen* als literarisches Zeugnis des Holocaust." In *Zeugenschaft des Holocaust: Zwischen Trauma, Tradierung und Ermittlung*. Edited by Michael Elm and Gottfried Kössler. Frankfurt: Campus Verlag, 2007.

Funkenstein, Amos. "The Incomprehensible Catastrophe: Memory and Narrative." In *The Narrative Study of Lives*, vol. 1. Edited by Ruthellen Josselson and Amia Lieblich. Newbury Park and London: Sage, 1993.

Fussell, Paul. *The Great War and Modern Memory*. New York: Oxford University Press, 1975.

Garbarini, Alexandra. *Numbered Days: Diaries and the Holocaust*. New Haven, CT: Yale University Press, 2006.

Gay, Peter. *Freud, Jews and Other Germans: Masters and Victims in Modernist Culture*. New York: Oxford University Press, 1978.

Gay, Peter. "Inside the Third Reich." *New York Times Book Review*, November 22, 1998.

Gay, Peter. *My German Question: Growing Up in Nazi Berlin*. New Haven, CT: Yale University Press, 1998.

Geertz, Clifford. *The Interpretation of Cultures: Selected Essays*. New York: Basic Books, 1973.

Geertz, Clifford. *Works and Lives: The Anthropologist as Author*. Stanford, CA: Stanford University Press, 1988.

Gellately, Robert. *The Gestapo and German Society: Enforcing Racial Policy 1933–1945*. Oxford: Clarendon Press, 1991.

Gellately, Robert. *Backing Hitler: Consent and Coercion in Nazi Germany*. Oxford: Oxford University Press, 2001.

Gerlach, Christian. *The Extermination of the European Jews*. Cambridge: Cambridge University Press, 2016.

Gerlach, Christian, and Götz Aly. *Das letzte Kapitel: Realpolitik, Ideologie und der Mord an den ungarischen Juden 1944–1945*. Stuttgart: Deutsche Verlags-Anstalt, 2002.

Gigliotti, Simone. *The Train Journey: Transit, Captivity, and Witnessing in the Holocaust*. New York: Berghahn Books, 2009.

Gilbert, Felix. *A European Past: Memoirs 1905–1945*. New York: Norton, 1988.

Glazar, Richard. *Trap with a Green Fence: Survival in Treblinka*. Translated by Roslyn Theoblad. Evanston, IL: Northwestern University Press, 1995.

Głowiński, Michał. *The Black Seasons*. Translated by Marci Shore. Evanston, IL: Northwestern University Press, 2005.

Goldhagen, Daniel Jonah. *Hitler's Willing Executioners: Ordinary Germans and the Holocaust*. New York: Knopf, 1996.

Gordon, Robert S. C. *Primo Levi's Ordinary Virtues: From Testimony to Ethics*. Oxford: Oxford University Press, 2001.

Gordon, Robert S. C., ed. *The Cambridge Companion to Primo Levi*. New York: Cambridge University Press, 2007.

Gourevitch, Philip. "The Memory Thief." *New Yorker*, June 14, 1999, pp. 48–68.

Grabowski, Jan. *Hunt for the Jews: Betrayal and Murder in German-Occupied Poland*. Bloomington: Indiana University Press, 2013.

Gross, Jan T. *Neighbors: The Destruction of the Jewish Community in Jedwabne*. Princeton, NJ: Princeton University Press, 2001.

Gross, Jan T. *Revolution from Abroad: The Soviet Conquest of Poland's Western Ukraine and Western Belorussia*. Expanded ed. Princeton, NJ: Princeton University Press, 2002.

Gross, Jan T. *Fear: Anti-Semitism in Poland after Auschwitz: An Essay in Historical Interpretation*. New York: Random House, 2006.

Gross, Jan T. "Opportunistic Killings and Plunder of Jews by Their Neighbors—A Norm or an Exception in German Occupied Europe?" In *Years of Persecution, Years of Extermination: Saul Friedländer and the Future of Holocaust Studies*. Edited by Christian Wiese and Paul Betts. London: Continuum, 2010.

Gross, Jan Tomasz, and Irena Grudzińska Gross. *Golden Harvest: Events on the Periphery of the Holocaust*. New York: Oxford University Press, 2012.

Gruner, Wolf. *Jewish Forced Labor under the Nazis*. New York: Cambridge University Press, 2006.

Gutman, Israel. "Social Stratification in the Concentration Camps." In *The Nazi Concentration Camps*. Edited by Yisrael Gutman and Avital Saf. Jerusalem: Yad Vashem, 1984.

Gutman, Yisrael. *The Jews of Warsaw 1939–1943*. Bloomington: Indiana University Press, 1994.

Gutman Yisrael, and Michael Berebaum, eds. *Anatomy of the Auschwitz Death Camp*. Bloomington: Indiana University Press, 1994.

Haffner, Sebastian. *Defying Hitler: A Memoir*. Translated by Oliver Pretzel. New York: Farrar, Straus and Giroux, 2002.

Halwachs, Maurice. *On Collective Memory*. Translated by Lewis A. Coser. Chicago: University of Chicago Press, 1992.

Hammermann, Gabrielle. "Die Todesmärche aus den Konzentrationslagern 1944/ 1945." In *Terror nach Innen: Verbrechen am Ende des Zweiten Weltkrieges*. Edited by Cord Arendes, Edgar Wolfram, and Jörg Zedler. Göttingen: Wallstein, 2006.

Harrowitz, Nancy. *Primo Levi and the Identity of a Survivor*. Toronto: University of Toronto Press, 2016.

Hart, Kitty. *I Am Alive*. London: Corgi, 1961.

Hart, Kitty. *Return to Auschwitz: The Remarkable Story of a Girl Who Survived the Holocaust*. London: Grafton, 1983.

Heer, Hannes, ed., *Im Herzen der Finsternis: Victor Klemperer als Chronist der NS-Zeit*. Berlin: Aufbau-Verlag, 1997.

Heim, Susanne Heim. "The German-Jewish Relationship in the Diaries of Victor Klemperer." In *Probing the Depths of German Antisemitism: German Society and the Persecution of the Jews, 1933–1941*. Edited by David Bankier. New York: Berghahn Books, 2000.

Herbert, Ulrich. *Hitler's Foreign Workers: Enforced Labor in Germany under the Third Reich*. Translated by William Templer. New York: Cambridge University Press, 1997.

Herbert, Ulrich, ed. *National Socialist Extermination Policies: Contemporary German Perspectives and Controversies*. New York: Berghahn Books, 2000.

Herf, Jeffrey. *Divided Memory: The Nazi Past in the Two Germanys*. Cambridge, MA: Harvard University Press, 1997.

Herf, Jeffrey. *The Jewish Enemy: Nazi Propaganda during World War II and the Holocaust*. Cambridge, MA: Harvard University Press, 2006.

Heyman, Éva. *The Diary of Éva Heyman*. Translated by Misha M. Kohn. New York: Shapolsky, 1988.

Hilberg, Raul. *Perpetrators Victims Bystanders: The Jewish Catastrophe 1933–1945*. New York: HarperCollins, 1992.

Hilberg, Raul. *The Destruction of the European Jews*. 3rd ed., 3 vols. New Haven, CT: Yale University Press, 2003.

Hirsch, Marianne. *Family Frames: Photography, Narrative, and Postmemory*. Cambridge, MA: Harvard University Press, 1997.

Hoffman, Eva. *After Such Knowledge: Memory, History, and the Legacy of the Holocaust*. New York: Public Affairs. 2004.

Horowitz, Sara. *Voicing the Void: Muteness and Memory in Holocaust Fiction*. Albany: State University of New York Press, 1997.

Horwitz, Gordon J. *Ghettostadt: Łódź and the Making of a Nazi City*. Cambridge, MA: Harvard University Press, 2008.

Hosenfeld, Wilm. *"Ich versuche jeden zu retten": Das Leben eines deutschen Offiziers in Briefen und Tagebüchern*. Edited by Thomas Vogel. Munich: Deutsche-Verlags Anstalt, 2004.

Howe, Irving. "How to Write about the Holocaust." *New York Review of Books*, March 28, 1985.

Hughes, H. Stuart. *Prisoners of Hope: The Silver Age of the Italian Jews 1924–1974*. Cambridge, MA: Harvard University Press, 1983.

Hughes, Judith M. *The Holocaust and the Revival of Psychological History*. New York: Cambridge University Press, 2015.

Jacobs, Peter. *Victor Klemperer: Im Kern ein deutsches Gewächs: Eine Biographie*. Berlin: Aufbau, 2000.

Jarausch, Konrad H., and Michael Geyer. *Shattered Past: Reconstructing German Histories*. Princeton, NJ: Princeton University Press, 2003.

Judt, Tony. *Postwar: A History of Europe since 1945*. New York: Penguin, 2005.

Judt, Tony. *Reappraisals: Reflections on the Forgotten Twentieth Century*. New York: Penguin, 2008.

Kaplan, Chaim A. *Scroll of Agony: The Warsaw Diary of Chaim A. Kaplan*. Edited and translated by Abraham I. Katsh. Bloomington: Indiana University Press, 1999.

Kaplan, Marion A. *Between Dignity and Despair: Jewish Life in Nazi Germany*. New York: Oxford University Press, 1998.

Karpf, Anne. *The War After: Living with the Holocaust*. London: Heinemann, 1996.

Kassow, Samuel D. *Who Will Write Our History? Emanuel Ringelblum, the Warsaw Ghetto, and the Oyneg Shabes Archive*. Bloomington: Indiana University Press, 2007.

Kershaw, Ian. *Popular Opinion and Political Dissent in the Third Reich: Bavaria 1933–1945*. Oxford: Oxford University Press, 1983.

Kershaw, Ian. *Hitler*. 2 vols. New York: Norton, 1999–2000.

Kershaw, Ian. *The Nazi Dictatorship: Problems and Perspectives of Interpretation*. 4th ed. New York: Oxford University Press, 2000.

Kershaw, Ian. *Hitler, the Germans, and the Final Solution*. New Haven, CT: Yale University Press, 2008.

Kershaw, Ian. *The End: The Defiance and Destruction of Hitler's Germany, 1944–45*. New York: Penguin, 2011.

Kertész, Imre. "Nobel Lecture 2002: Heureka." www.nobelprize.org/nobel_prizes/literature/laureates/2002/kertész-lecture-e.html.

Kertész, Imre. *Fatelessness*. Translated by Tim Wilkinson. New York: Vintage, 2004.

Kertész, Imre. *Kaddish for an Unborn Child*. Translated by Tim Wilkinson. New York: Random House, 2004.

Kertész, Imre. *Liquidation*. Translated by Tim Wilkinson. New York: Knopf, 2004.

Kertész, Imre. *Fiasco*. Translated by Tim Wilkinson. Brooklyn, NY: Melville House, 2011.

Kertész, Imre. *The Holocaust as Culture*. Translated by Thomas Cooper. London: Seagull Books, 2011.

Kertész, Imre. *Dossier K.* Translated by Tim Wilkinson. Brooklyn, NY: Melville House, 2013.

Klemperer, Victor. *Curriculum Vitae: Erinnerungen 1881–1918.* Edited by Walter Nowojski. 2 vols. Berlin: Aufbau-Verlag, 1996.

Klemperer, Victor. *Leben sammeln, nicht fragen wozu und warum.* Edited by Walter Nowojski, with the assistance of Christian Löser. 2 vols. Berlin: Aufbau-Verlag, 1996.

Klemperer, Victor. *I Will Bear Witness: A Diary of the Nazi Years 1933–1945.* Translated by Martin Chalmers. 2 vols. New York: Random House, 1998–99.

Klemperer, Victor. *The Lesser Evil: The Diaries of Victor Klemperer 1945–1959.* Abridged and translated by Martin Chalmers. London: Weidenfeld and Nicolson, 2003.

Klemperer, Victor. *The Language of the Third: LTI, Lingua Tertii Imperii: A Philologist's Notebook.* Translated by Martin Brady. London: Continuum, 2006.

Klüger, Ruth. *weiter leben: Eine Jugend.* Göttingen: Wallstein, 1992.

Klüger, Ruth. *Still Alive: A Holocaust Girlhood Remembered.* New York: Feminist Press, 2001.

Klüger, Ruth. *unterwegs verloren: Erinnerungen.* Vienna: Paul Zsolnay, 2008.

Klüger, Ruth. "The Future of Holocaust Literature." *German Studies Review* 37 (2014): 391–403.

Kogon, Eugen. *The Theory and Practice of Hell: German Concentration Camps and the System Behind Them.* Translated by Heinz Norden. New York: Farrar, Straus, 1950.

Kohut, Thomas August. *A German Generation: An Experiential History of the Twentieth Century.* New Haven, CT: Yale University Press, 2012.

Koonz, Claudia. *The Nazi Conscience.* Cambridge, MA: Harvard University Press, 2003.

Kühne, Thomas. *Belonging and Genocide: Hitler's Community, 1918–1945.* New Haven, CT: Yale University Press, 2010.

Kulka, Otto Dov. *Landscapes of the Metropolis of Death: Reflections on Memory and Imagination.* Translated by Ralph Mandel. Cambridge, MA: Harvard University Press, 2013.

Kulka, Otto Dov, and Eberhard Jäckel, eds. *The Jews in the Secret Nazi Reports on Popular Opinion in Germany, 1933–1945.* New Haven, CT: Yale University Press, 2010.

LaCapra, Dominick. *Representing the Holocaust: History, Theory, Trauma.* Ithaca, NY: Cornell University Press, 1994.

LaCapra, Dominick. *History and Memory after Auschwitz.* Ithaca, NY: Cornell University Press, 1998.

Lang, Berel. *The Future of the Holocaust: Between History and Memory*. Ithaca, NY: Cornell University Press, 1999.

Lang, Berel. *Post-Holocaust: Interpretation, Misinterpretation, and the Claims of History*. Bloomington: Indiana University Press, 2005.

Lang, Berel. *Primo Levi: The Matter of a Life*. New Haven, CT: Yale University Press, 2013.

Langbein, Hermann. *Against All Hope: Resistance in the Nazi Concentration Camps 1938–1945*. New York: Paragon House, 1994.

Langer, Lawrence L. *Versions of Survival: The Holocaust and the Human Spirit*. Albany: State University of New York Press, 1982.

Langer, Lawrence L. *Holocaust Testimonies: The Ruins of Memory*. New Haven, CT: Yale University Press, 1991.

Langer, Lawrence L. *Admitting the Holocaust: Collected Essays*. New York: Oxford University Press, 1995.

Langer, Lawrence L. *Preempting the Holocaust*. New Haven, CT: Yale University Press, 1998.

Langer, Lawrence L, ed. *Art from the Ashes: A Holocaust Anthology*. New York: Oxford University Press, 1995.

Lanzmann, Claude. *Shoah: Transcription of English Subtitles*. New York: Pantheon, 1985.

Laqueur, Walter. "Three Witnesses: The Legacy of Viktor Klemperer, Willy Cohen, and Richard Koch." *Holocaust and Genocide Studies* 10 (1996): 252–266.

Lasker-Wallfisch, Anita. *Inherit the Truth 1939–1945: The Documented Experiences of a Survivor of Auschwitz and Belsen*. London: Giles de la Mare, 1996.

Lejeune, Philippe. *Cher cahier …*. Paris: Gallimard, 1989.

Lejeune, Philippe. *On Autobiography*. Translated by Katherine Leary. Minneapolis: University of Minnesota Press, 1989.

Lengyel, Olga. *Five Chimneys: The Story of Auschwitz*. Translated by Clifford Coch and Paul P. Weiss. Chicago: Academy Chicago, 1995.

Levi, Primo. *The Voice of Memory: Interviews 1961–1987*. Edited by Marco Belpoliti and Robert Gordon. Translated by Robert Gordon. New York: New Press, 2001.

Levi, Primo. *The Complete Works of Primo Levi*. Edited by Ann Goldstein. 3 vols. New York: Liveright, 2015.

Levi, Primo, with Leonardo de Benedetti. *Auschwitz Report*. Edited by Robert S. C. Gordon. Translated by Judith Woolf. London: Verso, 2006.

Lewis, Helen. *A Time to Speak*. Belfast: Blackstaff, 1992.

Lipstadt, Deborah E. *Denying the Holocaust: The Growing Assault on Truth and Memory*. New York: Free Press, 1993.

Lipstadt, Deborah E. *The Eichmann Trial*. New York: Schocken, 2011.

Lipton, Eunice Lipton. "Survival Skills." *Women's Review of Books* 19.4 (January 2002): 11–12.

Livingston, Michael A. *The Fascists and the Jews of Italy: Mussolini's Race Laws, 1938–1943*. New York: Cambridge University Press, 2014.

Longerich, Peter. *"Davon haben wir nichts gewusst!": Die Deutschen und die Judenverfolgung 1933–1945*. Munich: Siedler, 2006.

Longerich, Peter. *Holocaust: The Nazi Persecution and Murder of the Jews*. Oxford: Oxford University Press, 2010.

Lorenz, Dagmar C. G. "Memory and Criticism: Ruth Klüger's weiter leben." *Women in German Yearbook* 9 (1993): 207–224.

Loridan-Ivens, Marceline, with Judith Perrignon. *But You Did Not Come Back: A Memoir*. Translated by Sandra Smith. New York: Atlantic Monthly Press, 2016.

Losowick, Yaacov. *Hitler's Bureaucrats: The Nazi Security Police and the Banality of Evil*. Translated by Haim Watzman. London: Continuum, 2002.

Lower, Wendy. *The Diary of Samuel Golfard and the Holocaust in Galicia*. Lanham, MD: AltaMira, 2011.

Luzzatto, Sergio. *Primo Levi's Resistance: Rebels and Collaborators in Occupied Italy*. Translated by Frederika Randall. New York: Metropolitan, 2016.

Mahlendorf, Ursula. *The Shame of Survival: Working through a Nazi Childhood*. University Park: Pennsylvania State University Press, 2009.

Maier, Charles S. *The Unmasterable Past: History, Holocaust, and German National Identity*. Cambridge, MA: Harvard University Press, 1988.

Maliszewski, Paul. "A Whiff of Turnip Soup." *Times Literary Supplement*, August 19, 2005.

Mallon, Thomas. *A Book of One's Own: People and Their Diaries*. New York: Ticknor and Fields, 1984.

Marrus, Michael R. *The Holocaust in History*. Hanover, NH: University Press of New England, 1987.

Marrus, Michael R., and Robert O. Paxton. *Vichy France and the Jews*. New York: Basic Books, 1981.

Masurovsky, Marc. "Visualizing the Evacuations from the Auschwitz-Birkenau Camp System: When Does an Evacuation Turn into a Death March?" In *Freilungen: Auf den Spuren der Todesmärsche*. Edited by Jean-Luc Blondel, Susanne Urban, and Sebastian Schönemann. Göttingen: Wallstein, 2012.

Mazower, Mark. *Hitler's Empire: How the Nazis Ruled Europe*. New York: Penguin, 2008.

Mendelsohn, Daniel. *The Lost: A Search for Six of Six Million*. New York: HarperCollins, 2006.

Mendelsohn, Erza. *The Jews of East Central Europe between the World Wars.* Bloomington: Indiana University Press, 1983.

Miller, J. Hillis. *The Conflagration of Community: Fiction before and after Auschwitz.* Chicago: University of Chicago Press, 2011.

Moseley, Marcus. "Jewish Autobiography: The Elusive Subject." *Jewish Quarterly Review* 95 (2005): 16–59.

Némirovsky, Irène. *Suite française.* Translated by Sandra Smith. London: Chatto and Windus, 2006.

Niewyk, Donald, ed. *Fresh Wounds: Early Narratives of Holocaust Survival.* Chapel Hill: University of North Carolina Press, 1998.

Novick, Peter. *The Holocaust in American Life.* Boston: Houghton Mifflin, 1999.

Ofer, Dalia, and Lenore J. Weitzman, eds. *Women in the Holocaust.* New Haven, CT: Yale University Press, 1998.

Olney, James. *Metaphors of Self: The Meaning of Autobiography.* Princeton, NJ: Princeton University Press, 1972.

Olney, James. *Memory and Narrative: The Weave of Life-Writing.* Chicago: University of Chicago Press, 1998.

Olney, James, ed. *Autobiography: Essays Theoretical and Critical.* Princeton, NJ: Princeton University Press, 1980.

Olney, James, ed. *Studies in Autobiography.* New York: Oxford University Press, 1988.

Parks, Tim. "The Mystery of Primo Levi." *New York Review of Books*, November 5, 2015.

Patterson, David. *Sun Turned to Darkness: Memory and Recovery in the Holocaust Memoir.* Syracuse, NY: Syracuse University Press, 1998.

Patterson, David. *Along the Edge of Annihilation: The Collapse and Recovery of Life in the Holocaust Diary.* Seattle: University of Washington Press, 1999.

Paulsson, Gunnar S. *Secret City: The Hidden Jews of Warsaw 1940–1945.* New Haven, CT: Yale University Press, 2002.

Pohl, Dieter. "Die Holocaust Forschung und Goldhagens Thesen." *Vierteljahreshefte für Zeitgeschichte* 45 (1997): 12–48.

Polonsky, Antony, and Joanna B. Michlic, eds. *The Neighbors Respond: The Controversy over the Jedwabne Massacre in Poland.* Princeton, NJ: Princeton University Press, 2004.

Porter, Anna. *The Kasztner Train: The True Story of an Unknown Hero of the Holocaust.* New York: Walker, 2007.

Powell, Lawrence N. "Auschwitz: The Counterlife." *The Nation*, April 9, 2001.

Rabinovici, Doron. *Eichmann's Jews: The Jewish Administration in Holocaust Vienna, 1938–1945.* Translated by Nick Somers. Cambridge: Polity, 2011.

Reich-Ranicki, Marcel. *The Author of Himself: The Life of Marcel Reich-Ranicki*.
    Translated by Ewald Osers. Princeton, NJ: Princeton University Press, 2001.

Renza, Louis A. "The Veto of the Imagination: A Theory of Autobiography." *New
    Literary History* (1977): 1–26.

Ringelblum, Emmanuel. *Notes from the Warsaw Ghetto: The Journal of Emmanuel
    Ringelblum*. Edited and translated by Jacob Sloan. New York: McGraw-Hill, 1958.

Roseman, Mark. *A Past in Hiding: Memory and Survival in Nazi Germany*.
    New York: Henry Holt, 2000.

Roseman, Mark. "Contexts and Contradictions: Writing the Biography of a Holocaust
    Survivor." In *Biography between Structure and Agency: Central European Lives in
    International Historiography*. Edited by Volker R. Berghahn and Simone Lässig.
    New York: Berghahn Books, 2008.

Rosenfeld, Alvin H. *The End of the Holocaust*. Bloomington: Indiana University Press,
    2011.

Roth, Philip. "Conversation with Primo Levi." In *Survival in Auschwitz*, by Primo
    Levi. Translated by Stuart Woolf. New York: Simon and Schuster, 1996.

Rousso, Henry. *The Vichy Syndrome: History and Memory in France since 1944*.
    Translated by Arthur Goldhammer. Cambridge, MA: Harvard University Press,
    1991.

Rozett, Robert. *Conscripted Slaves: Hungarian Jewish Forced Laborers on the Eastern
    Front during the Second World War*. Jerusalem: Yad Vashem, 2013.

Safrian, Hans. *Eichmann's Men*. Translated by Ute Stargardt. New York: Cambridge
    University Press, 2010.

Salton, George Lucius, with Anna Salton Eisen. *The 23rd Psalm: A Holocaust Memoir*.
    Madison: University of Wisconsin Press, 2002.

Sands, Philippe. *East West Street: On the Origins of Genocide and Crimes against
    Humanity*. London: Weidenfeld and Nicolson, 2016.

Schleunes, Karl A. *The Twisted Road to Auschwitz: Nazi Policy toward German Jews
    1933–1939*. Urbana: University of Illinois Press, 1970.

Schmid, John. "An East German Publishing Coup." *New York Times*, October 7, 1996.

Schulte-Sasse, Linda, "'Living on' in the American Press: Ruth Kluger's 'Still Alive'
    and Its Challenge to a Cherished Holocaust Paradigm." *German Studies Review* 27
    (2004): 469–475.

Sebastian, Mihail. *Journal 1935–1944: The Fascist Years*. Edited by Radu Ioanid.
    Translated by Patrick Camiller. Chicago: Ivan R. Dee, 2000.

Segev, Tom. *The Seventh Million: The Israelis and the Holocaust*. Translated by Haim
    Watzman. New York: Hill and Wang, 1993.

Seidman, Naomi. "Elie Wiesel and the Scandal of Jewish Rage." *Jewish Social Studies*
    3 (1996): 1–19.

Semprún, Jorge. *The Long Voyage*. Translated by Richard Seaver. New York: Grove Press, 1964.

Sereny, Gitta. *Albert Speer: His Battle with Truth*. New York: Vintage, 1996.

Sereny, Gitta. *The Healing Wound: Experiences and Reflections on Germany, 1938–2001*. New York: Norton, 2001.

Shandley, Robert R., ed. *Unwilling Germans? The Goldhagen Debate*. Minneapolis: University of Minnesota Press, 1998.

Snyder, Timothy. *Bloodlands: Europe between Hitler and Stalin*. New York: Basic Books, 2010.

Snyder, Timothy. *Black Earth: The Holocaust as History and Warning*. New York: Tim Duggan, 2015.

Sodi, Risa, and Millicent Marcus, eds. *New Reflections on Primo Levi: Before and after Auschwitz*. New York: Palgrave Macmillan, 2011.

Sofsky, Wolfgang. *The Order of Terror: The Concentration Camp*. Translated by William Templer. Princeton, NJ: Princeton University Press, 1997.

Speer, Albert. *Inside the Third Reich: Memoirs*. Translated by Richard and Clara Winston. New York: Macmillan, 1970.

Stangneth, Bettina. *Eichmann Before Jerusalem*. New York: Knopf, 2014.

Stargardt, Nicholas. *Witnesses of War: Children's Lives under the Nazis*. New York: Knopf, 2006.

Stargardt, Nicholas. *The German War: A Nation under Arms, 1939–1945*. New York: Basic Books, 2015.

Steinberg, Paul. *Speak You Also: A Survivor's Reckoning*. Translated by Linda Coverdale. New York: Picador, 2000.

Steiner, George. *Language and Silence: Essays 1958–1966*. London: Faber and Faber, 1967.

Steinlauf, Michael C. *Bondage to the Dead: Poland and the Memory of the Holocaust*. Syracuse, NY: Syracuse University Press, 1997.

Steinweis, Alan E. *Kristallnacht 1938*. Cambridge, MA: Harvard University Press, 2009.

Stone, Dan. *Histories of the Holocaust*. New York: Oxford University Press, 2010.

Stone, Dan. *The Liberation of the Camps: The End of the Holocaust and Its Aftermath*. New Haven, CT: Yale University Press, 2015.

Szirtes, George. "Who Is Imre Kertész?" *Times Literary Supplement*, October 18, 2002.

Szpilman, Wladyslaw. *The Pianist: The Extraordinary True Story of One Man's Survival in Warsaw, 1939–1945*. Translated by Anthea Bell. New York: Picador, 1999.

Tarrow, Susan. "Remembering Primo Levi: A Conversation with 'Il Pikolo del Kommando 98." *Forum Italicum: Journal of Italian Studies* 28 (1994): 101–110.

Tec, Nechama. *Dry Tears: The Story of a Lost Childhood*. New York: Oxford University Press, 1984.

Tec, Nechama. *When the Light Pierced the Darkness: Christian Rescue of Jews in Nazi-Occupied Poland*. New York: Oxford University Press, 1986.

Tec, Nechama. *Resilience and Courage: Women, Men, and the Holocaust*. New Haven, CT: Yale University Press, 2003.

Thomson, Ian. *Primo Levi*. London: Hutchison, 2002.

Todorov, Tzvetan. *Facing the Extreme: Moral Life in the Concentration Camps*. Translated by Arthur Denner and Abigail Pollak. New York: Henry Holt, 1996.

Tooze, Adam. *The Wages of Destruction: The Making and Breaking of the Nazi Economy*. London: Allen Lane, 2006.

Tory, Avraham. *Surviving the Holocaust: The Kovno Ghetto Diary*. Edited by Martin Gilbert. Translated by Jerzy Michalowicz. Cambridge, MA: Harvard University Press, 1990.

Traverso, Paola. "Victor Klemperers Deutschlandbild—Ein jüdisches Tagebuch? *Tel Aviver Jahrbuch für Deutsche Geschichte* 26 (1997): 307–344.

Trunk, Isaiah. *Judenrat: The Jewish Councils in Eastern Europe under Nazi Occupation*. New York: Macmillan, 1972.

Trunk, Isaiah. *Łódź Ghetto: A History*. Bloomington: Indiana University Press, 2006.

Turner, Henry Ashby, Jr. "Victor Klemperer's Holocaust." *German Studies Review* 22 (1999): 385–395.

Vági, Zoltán, László Csősz, and Gábor Kádár, eds. *The Holocaust in Hungary: Evolution of a Genocide*. Lanham, MD: AltaMira, 2013.

Vasvári, Louise O., and Steven Tötösy de Zepetnek, eds. *Imre Kertész and Holocaust Literature*. West Lafayette, IN: Purdue University Press, 2005.

Wachsmann, Nikolaus. *kl: A History of the Nazi Concentration Camps*. New York: Farrar, Straus and Giroux, 2015.

Wasserstein, Bernard. *On the Eve: The Jews of Europe before the Second World War*. New York: Simon and Schuster, 2012.

Watt, Roderick H. "'Landsersprache, Heeressprache, Nazisprache?' Victor Klemperer and Werner Krauss on the Linguistic Legacy of the Third Reich." *Modern Language Review* 95 (2000): 424–436.

Waxman, Zoë Vania. *Writing the Holocaust: Identity, Testimony, Representation*. Oxford: Oxford University Press, 2006.

Wiesel, Elie. *Night*. Translated by Marion Wiesel. New York: Hill and Wang, 2006.

Wieviorka, Annette. *The Era of the Witness*. Translated by Jared Stark. Ithaca, NY: Cornell University Press, 2006.

Wilkomirski, Binjamin. *Fragments: Memories of a Childhood, 1939–1948*. Translated by Carol Brown Janeway. New York: Schocken, 1996.

Wisse, Ruth, ed. *Holocaust Chronicles: Individualizing the Holocaust*. Hoboken, NJ: Ktav, 1999.

Wood, James. "The Art of Witness: How Primo Levi Survived." *New Yorker*, September 28, 2015, pp. 68–75.

Wyschogrod, Edith. *An Ethics of Remembering: History, Heterology, and the Nameless Others*. Chicago: University of Chicago Press, 1998.

Yerushalmi, Yosef Hayim. *Zakhor: Jewish History and Jewish Memory*. Seattle: University of Washington Press, 1982.

Young, James E. "Interpreting Literary Testimony: A Preface to Rereading Holocaust Diaries and Memoirs." *New Literary History* 18 (1987): 403–423.

Young, James E. *Writing and Rewriting the Holocaust: Narrative and the Consequences of Interpretation*. Bloomington: Indiana University Press, 1988.

Young, James E. *The Texture of Memory: Holocaust Memorials and Meaning*. New Haven, CT: Yale University Press, 1993.

Zsolt, Béla. *Nine Suitcases: A Memoir*. Translated by Ladislaus Löb. New York: Schocken Books, 2004.

Zuckerman, Yitzhak. *A Surplus of Memory: Chronicle of the Warsaw Ghetto Uprising*. Translated by Barbara Harshav. Berkeley: University of California Press, 1993.

Index